Praise

HOW TO TALK
SO YOUR KIDS
WILL LISTEN

I have learned more basic communication skills with my
children from this one book than any book I have ever read on
the subject. Norm Wright knows how to deliver practicality
and commonsense parenting at its best.

JIM BURNS, PH.D.
AUTHOR, THE TEN BUILDING BLOCKS FOR A HAPPY FAMILY
PRESIDENT, YOUTHBUILDERS

Now is the time to turn up the frequency and get in tune with
our children and teens. *How to Talk So Your Kids Will Listen* offers
biblically sound, practical techniques on how to overcome
parent-child communication differences. Norm Wright's
real-life examples and hands-on approach encourage parents
to step out in confidence and exert positive control
over those differences.

JOSH D. MCDOWELL
AUTHOR, CHILDREN DEMAND A VERDICT *AND* HOW TO BE
A HERO TO YOUR KIDS
SPEAKER

HOW TO TALK
SO YOUR
KIDS WILL
LISTEN

Dr. H. Norman Wright

Regal

From Gospel Light
Ventura, California, U.S.A.

PUBLISHED BY REGAL BOOKS
FROM GOSPEL LIGHT
VENTURA, CALIFORNIA, U.S.A.
PRINTED IN THE U.S.A.

Regal Books is a ministry of Gospel Light, a Christian publisher dedicated to serving the local church. We believe God's vision for Gospel Light is to provide church leaders with biblical, user-friendly materials that will help them evangelize, disciple and minister to children, youth and families.

It is our prayer that this Regal book will help you discover biblical truth for your own life and help you meet the needs of others. May God richly bless you.

For a free catalog of resources from Regal Books/Gospel Light, please call your Christian supplier or contact us at 1-800-4-GOSPEL *or* www.regalbooks.com.

Cover design by Robert Williams
Interior design by Stephen Hahn
Edited by Amy Spence

Library of Congress Cataloging-in-Publication Data

Wright, H. Norman.
  How to talk so your kids will listen / H. Norman Wright.
     p. cm.
  Includes bibliographical references.
  ISBN 0-8307-3328-0
  1. Child rearing–Religious aspects–Christianity. 2. Communication in the family–Religious aspects–Christianity. 3. Parent and child–Religious aspects–Christianity. I. Title.
  BV4529.W735 2004
  649.1–dc22   2003025867

1   2   3   4   5   6   7   8   9   10   11   12   13   14   15   /   10   09   08   07   06   05   04

Rights for publishing this book in other languages are contracted by Gospel Light Worldwide, the international nonprofit ministry of Gospel Light. Gospel Light Worldwide also provides publishing and technical assistance to international publishers dedicated to producing Sunday School and Vacation Bible School curricula and books in the languages of the world. For additional information, visit www.gospellightworldwide.org; write to Gospel Light Worldwide, P.O. Box 3875, Ventura, CA 93006; or send an e-mail to info@gospellightworldwide.org.

Contents

Discover Your Child's Uniqueness

It's too bad there isn't a beatitude for parents that says, "Blessed is the flexible parent, for he or she will have the greatest opportunity to communicate with his or her child." Every child is unique. Each one is different. This is the way it should be. It is the way God created us.

When children are born, they come with an inheritance. It comes from the gene pool of each parent. It might not be seen at first, but it gradually unfolds. If you have three children, it's as though you picked up one from Target, one from Nordstrom and one from JCPenney. They're all different, aren't they? Each child *thinks* differently, *acts* differently and *communicates* differently. Read how some parents describe their children:

- "My daughter is a real space cadet. Sometimes I wonder what she uses for a brain."
- "My son has a big mouth. He's loud and goes on and on."
- "I think my daughter is a hermit. I just can't understand why she's so quiet."
- "My son can get lost between his bedroom and the

kitchen, especially when I ask him to do something."
- "My daughter talks first and thinks later."
- "My kid is so picky. He'll ask me the time, and I'll say, 'Oh, around four o'clock.' Then he'll say, 'No, I want the exact time.' What a pain."
- "My daughter is so absentminded. She seems to be thinking about too many things at the same time."
- "My daughter is way too sensitive. She always gets her feelings hurt."
- "I wonder if my son has any feelings. He always has to be right, even when it makes his friends dislike him. But he doesn't seem to care."
- "My son is only seven. But even now he has a place for everything, and he isn't satisfied unless everything is in its place before he goes to bed at night. Me? I let everything lie where it falls. But does he ever get after me about that!"
- "My teenage daughter is a procrastinator. She gets her work done eventually, but her last minute antics disrupt the whole family."
- "I try to talk to my son, but he always changes the subject in the middle of the conversation. I sometimes wonder if his brain is stuck in neutral."

Did you notice some of the words used to describe the children—"space cadet," "big mouth," "loud," "hermit," "lost," "talks first and thinks later," "picky," "too sensitive," "procrastinator," "changes the subject"? Do these words sound negative or positive? Are these traits you would want to change in your child, or could you accept them? What if each trait or characteristic is the way God uniquely created your child, and it's your task to understand your child?

UNIQUE BEHAVIORS AND PERSONALITIES

Children have quirks of behavior and personality that at times irritate their parents. Yet in most cases the problem isn't that children are bad, it's simply that their responses and thought patterns are *different* from their parents'.

You get frustrated because you can't understand why your child isn't more like you. Trying to change your child's personality to match yours is as pointless and futile as trying to change your child's physical features to make him or her look like you. The key to reducing your frustration over your child's quirks of behavior, and to communicate with him or her, is to understand and accommodate your child's unique personality style.

Every child is predisposed toward certain personality characteristics. These leanings reflect his or her genetic inheritance, birth order and early environment. A child's personality traits direct his or her preferences for responding to life and his or her communication style—much like a child's handedness directs his or her preference for completing manual tasks. For instance, just because a child is right-handed, doesn't mean the child never uses his or her left hand. The child may prefer his or her right hand strongly, rarely using his or her left hand. Or the child may be more ambidextrous and use his or her left hand for several tasks. The more the child practices his or her handedness preference, the more the child relies on it with confidence. Similarly, the more a child responds in line with his or her personality predisposition, the stronger that style becomes in the child.[1]

In Psalm 139:14 (*NIV*), read King David's words: "I praise you because I am fearfully and wonderfully made; your works are wonderful." Christians believe that every person is made in the image of God and is of infinite worth and value. Every person is unique. Yet most parents find it much easier to value the aspects of their children that are similar to their own. I've heard parents remark, "Tommy is just like me, but I'm not sure where Jill came from. She is so different from the rest of us."

Unique Differences

What is the first thing that comes to mind when you hear the word "different"? Are the meanings you associate with "different" primarily positive or negative? If I were to approach you on the street and say, "You sure look different today," would you think I was giving you a compliment and reply, "Well, thank you very much," or would you think that I was being critical?

Every person is different. Yet often those differences are not understood or valued by others.

"Different" suggests a deviation from some kind of standard or norm. It suggests that something is not quite the way it usually is or the way it should be. Many people interpret "different" to mean "unusual, inappropriate, inferior or wrong." If I said, "You sure look like a deviate," you would know that I was being negative and critical.

On the other hand, what do you think of when you hear the word "unique" or "special"? Do you tend to have a more positive response to those terms? Every person is different. Yet often those differences are not understood or valued by others.

Replicated scientific research has shown that infants show significant individual differences from birth. We know that infants are born with unique temperamental characteristics, behavior traits and ways of responding to external stimuli. Some distinguishing characteristics include their ability levels, needs and feelings. Because every infant has a unique way of interacting with his or her environment, every parent must understand and relate to the infant's uniqueness.

Intelligence Differences

Children come with different personalities and different types of intelligence. Are you aware of the eight kinds of intelligence, and the fact that each child is born with a unique distribution of each? Some of these intelligence types may surprise you:

1. Some children have strong *emotional intelligence* and have a unique ability to establish and maintain healthy relationships with others and themselves. They're able to handle feelings and empathize.
2. Those who have strong *academic intelligence* do well in school, for they can sit, listen, learn, absorb and comprehend. Yet it doesn't mean they can apply all this knowledge or use it constructively in life.
3. There is *physical intelligence*. These children do well at sports, as well as maintain their bodies in a positive way.
4. Some children are gifted with *creative intelligence* and have a more developed imagination. When the imagination is stimulated, it grows. They often think differently, are more original and create in their own way.
5. Other children have *artistic intelligence* and are interested in drawing, writing, acting, singing, playing an instrument and so on.

6. *Commonsense intelligence* reflects children who want the practical rather than the intellectual. They want what is relevant and useful. They want to apply what works.

7. *Intuitive intelligence* is seen in children who just know things. Information simply comes to them rather than being taught or told. They have a sixth sense and can understand information without having to study all the details.

8. Some children have *gifted intelligence*. They are good at certain types of intelligence, but not as good at others. It seems that all their eggs end up in one basket. They may need to develop their special skills, as well as get help for the other kinds of intelligence.

In which of these types of intelligence is your child gifted? Remember that two children who are gifted in the same area of intelligence will reflect it differently because of variables such as personality and environment. For example, what if one child is an extrovert and the other child is an introvert?

Most important, if a child focuses only on his or her strengths, the child misses out on other parts of life, which creates imbalance. Our task as parents is not to fall into the trap of encouraging our children's strength alone but to encourage other areas as well.

Learning Differences

Children are different in other ways such as speed of learning. For example, it seems that some children possess their type of intelligence from birth. They are born with their one or two areas of giftedness already developed. Other children may be gradual learners, while some children are late bloomers.

Some people call children who fall into one of these three kinds of learning runners, walkers and jumpers:

1. A *runner* is given a new task and understands it immediately. This child learns quickly, but to stay interested and involved, he or she needs to be challenged.

2. A *walker* takes longer to learn but responds well to instruction. This child seems to learn a little, gets better and then lets you know he or she is learning. Encouragement does wonders for a walker.

3. A *jumper* is usually a challenge for parents. This child takes a long time to learn, and you may wonder if he or she is ever going to get it. Yes, this child takes instruction, but he or she doesn't seem to show any signs of learning. You wonder if your jumper is listening. You teach the child again and again, but he or she doesn't seem to get it. Again and again you go over his or her homework, how to feed the dog or how to greet people, but the child keeps forgetting. You wonder, *Where is my child's head right now?* You wonder if anything is getting through, but then one day it clicks. You had no idea. Unfortunately, what hinders a jumper from learning is the parent or teacher who gives up on the child.

Some children are runners in one area and jumpers in another area. And in the area where the child is a jumper, he or she may be uncooperative and resistant, but that doesn't mean the child is low in this area of intelligence. It could be the area in which the child has his or her greatest strength. In addition, just because the child is a runner in one area, doesn't mean he or she will excel in that area. The easiest path does not always correlate with the area of greatest strength.

If your first child is a runner and your second child is a jumper, your challenge is not to compare the two children but to discover each child's uniqueness, encourage each child's growth and reinforce that growth. Your communication with each child will need to be adapted. Remember that it is easy to be frustrated with a jumper and resort to critical and negative comments.[2]

CHILDREN'S COMMUNICATION NEEDS

One of the most important aspects of communicating is *knowing your child or teen*. Your effectiveness in communicating will be in direct proportion to the extent that you know your child.

Let's consider some children who are different or unique in contrast to one another. Remember, you will need to talk differently to each child in order to connect. Within each type described, all children will differ.

Karen—the Outgoing, Bubbly Child

Even at 10 years of age, Karen is an outgoing, bubbly child. She knows a lot of children at school and in her neighborhood, and she wouldn't think of doing something without getting some of her friends involved. Her parents often say, "Why don't you just sit home and play by yourself for a while?" But being alone doesn't sound like much fun to Karen. Whenever her parents require her to be quiet and reflective and to work by herself, Karen tends to procrastinate. She gets her stimulation from being involved with people and doing things.

Karen is like a solar panel. When she has to be alone, she feels like she is under a heavy cloud cover. A solar panel needs to be in the sun to get its energy; therefore, Karen needs to be around people. Sometimes she gets so recharged that it's hard for her to slow down.

People usually know what Karen is thinking because she often talks to herself out loud. Her parents frequently say, "Karen, who are you talking to? Why don't you be quiet for a change? Give our ears a rest!" Even at school she is one of the first children to raise her hand when the teacher asks a question. She may not know the answer at first, but in the process of talking about it, the answer often comes to her mind.[3]

There's something else about Karen: She seems to be secure and self-confident. She's gregarious and outgoing, but she won't believe she's done a good job unless she hears it from someone else. *She has a high need for compliments and affirmation* (that's

Your effectiveness in communicating will be in direct proportion to the extent that you know your child.

important to remember). Karen may ask you again and again what you think of a task she's done if she doesn't hear it from you. Karen wants you to notice and comment.

Does Karen sound like anyone you know? Perhaps you're like this, or you may be the exact opposite. Let's review the characteristics of Karen and learn the best ways to communicate with her:

- Karen tends to talk first and think later. She doesn't know what to say until she hears herself saying it. She needs the freedom to formulate her thoughts out loud, although there will be times when you think, *Can't she ever be quiet?*

- Karen tends to speak louder and faster; she is more animated. She brainstorms out loud for the whole world to hear whether others are listening or not. Remember, her ideas are just her brainstorming. It doesn't mean this is what she is going to do. Don't ever react. Just say, "Are you brainstorming out loud again?" and "Tell me more."

- Karen knows a lot of people and believes most of them are her "close friends." She'll want a party for 30 of her close friends. Help her to select her truly close friends. Limits are all right.

- Karen doesn't mind reading or having a conversation while the TV or radio is on in the background; in fact, she may be oblivious to this "distraction." She can handle it.

- Karen is approachable and easily engaged by friends and strangers alike. Your words, "Don't ever talk to strangers," are difficult to follow when your child is young. You will need to teach Karen about appropriate boundaries.

- Sometimes Karen exaggerates and shares too openly about personal things—even about what you do as parents. This is where you may need to teach what is appropriate to share and what is not.

- Karen likes any and all social events and talks with as many people as possible.

- Karen finds listening more difficult than talking; she doesn't like to give up the limelight. Teach her to listen by both modeling listening and teaching her to give others the same opportunity.

- Karen may talk louder and faster and knows that if she can "just say one more thing" the whole issue will be cleared up. This makes conflict resolution difficult.
- This one is *very important*. Karen may think she's done a good job, but she won't believe it until she hears it from someone else. She has a high need for verbal affirmation. Give her affirmation and compliments even when you think you've given enough.

John—the Quiet, Shy Child

Consider another child who is also unique. John is different from Karen in many ways. He loves to spend time playing by himself or reading in his room. He seems to thrive on peace and quiet. He's learned to concentrate quite well in most settings, since it isn't always easy for him to find the space or solitude that he wants. He's a good listener, so other kids and adults like him. But they also see John as shy, reserved and reflective.

John has two close friends; he doesn't like large groups very much. He usually is hesitant the first day of school or in other new settings. New people, situations or events are not welcomed by John. He enjoys group activities like church camp when his friends attend with him, but getting involved in a large group alone doesn't appeal to him very much. John's parents wonder why he seems to be antisocial, even with them. When he comes home from a group activity, he heads for his room instead of sharing what happened. They don't understand that he needs peace and quiet to recharge his batteries, which have been depleted by the stress of being with a lot of people. People drain him. An analogy to a battery may be useful to understand this concept. When a battery is attached to a charge, energy is flowing into the battery. When the battery is powering a lightbulb, energy is flowing out of the battery.

Energy flows *into* children like Karen when they are around people. Energy flows *out* of children like Karen when they are quietly reflecting on issues. This type of person is called an extrovert. In sharp contrast, energy flows *into* children like John when they are able to reflect quietly. Energy flows *out* of children like John when they interact with others. They need to stop and rest to get their energy back. This type of person is called an introvert.

Sometimes it's difficult to get an immediate response from John. He likes to say, "Let me think about it" or "I'll tell you later." This often frustrates his parents, especially his dad who is an extrovert. John likes to rehearse what he's going to say in his head before he says it. When he does speak, John likes to share his thoughts and feelings without interruption. Sometimes he gets upset at others who tend to butt in and even finish some of his sentences for him. He may take 5 to 10 seconds before responding to a question.

Occasionally John's deliberateness works against him in school. Some of his teachers wonder if he's mentally slow. They unfairly compare him to the extroverts in class who have their hand in the air while the question is still being asked. However, when all the students are asked to think about a problem for 20 seconds and then to respond, John's hand is one of the first to fly into the air. He's not slow by any means. He's more of a stealth person who runs deep and silent.

When John has a teacher who bases part of his or her grade on classroom participation, he's at a disadvantage. If he has a project at school or church that requires him to make a presentation to the group, he usually puts off preparing for it and working on it until he is forced into it. It doesn't do any good to admonish him by saying, "Just go ahead and speak up; you can do it." He's very uncomfortable in front of people.[4]

Does John sound like anyone you know? Perhaps you're like this, or you may be the exact opposite. Let's review the characteristics of John to learn the best ways to communicate with him:

- John carries on great conversations with himself: what the other person might say, and then what he might say, and then what the other person might say and so on. He does this so realistically that he believes the conversation actually occurred. You can imagine what misunderstandings this can cause, even in the family!
- John may be suspicious of compliments. In turn, he may be sparse in giving them. An introvert child does not like being the center of attention, so giving John a compliment in front of 30 children may make him uncomfortable. He also feels drained by having his physical space invaded. He doesn't like to share a room or have someone sitting too close to him.
- John rehearses things before saying them and probably prefers that others do the same. John needs to think to speak. In fact, he may take between 5 to 10 seconds before responding. He's not ignoring you; he's thinking. When you ask him a question say, "Here's something I'd like you to think about and then let's talk about it" or "Tonight at our family gathering we're going to talk about [insert topic]. I thought you would like to know in advance."
- John enjoys the peace and quiet of having time to himself. He finds his private time too easily invaded and tends to adapt by developing a *high power of concentration* that can shut out TV, noisy siblings or nearby conversations. Do you ever feel tuned out? It will happen.
- John is perceived as a great listener, but he may feel that

others take advantage of him. He also needs patient people around him and may feel overwhelmed in a group of people like Karen. They drain him.

- Some people think John is shy, but he is not. When he's with someone he's comfortable with, he can talk on and on.
- Sometimes people think John is not interested or tuned in because he does not say anything. However, he is saying a lot—in his head, not out loud like Karen.
- John prefers to share special occasions with just one other person or a few close friends. Large family gatherings can be draining, even as a child.
- John likes to state his thoughts or feelings without interruption. If interrupted, John can lose his place and has to exert more energy to get his thoughts back in order. You will need to talk to him in a nonpressured environment. You should not be intense or loud in your conversation; it will turn him off. Use gentle, probing questions and suggest that it's okay to think about his answers for a while before responding. And when he's ready to speak, John needs you to listen attentively without interrupting.
- John needs to recharge alone after he has spent time socializing with a group of people. Big, long parties at school or a week at camp in a dorm with no privacy is too much. He needs small gatherings.
- John gets suspicious if people are too complimentary; he needs less verbal feedback. He prefers that feedback be given in private.

Part of the difficulty in communication between parent and child occurs when you as a parent are the opposite of your child. Perhaps you are like Karen, an extrovert, but your child is an introvert, like John. (About 70 percent of people in our society are extroverts.)[5] "Extrovert" and "introvert" are familiar terms, but often they are not fully understood or accepted by some people. Remember, there is nothing wrong with being one or the other. Additionally, some children will be very extreme in one direction, while others seem to have a blend of the two.

You don't have to feel like a bad parent if you can't keep up with your extrovert child.

Differences Between Parent and Child

Sometimes it is difficult to adjust to a child that is your opposite. At times, an introvert parent can feel as if his or her extrovert child is both a joy and a curse, and vice versa. Being different is a wonderful opportunity to teach your child about individual differences and how to accept them. Let your extrovert child know that you as a parent can be drained by too much going on, and that you need breaks to recharge your energy in a way your child may not. Tell him or her that you want to be involved in their activities, but don't hesitate to set limits. Some introvert parents tell their extrovert children that they can attend two sports events a month, but that's their limit. You don't have to feel like a bad parent if you can't keep up with your extrovert child.

Some parents teach their children about extrovert and introvert differences so that they are more aware of their tendencies, as well as other people's tendencies.

The author of *The Introvert Advantage* says:

> At the dinner table make sure all the children have a turn
> to talk. Introverts feel uncomfortable about interrupt-
> ing, so they may not join a family discussion. If they
> know they are going to have a turn, they can have time
> to prepare their thoughts. Help the talkers learn to wait
> for their slower-paced brother or sister. Don't let one sib-
> ling interrupt or talk for another. It's obvious that no
> child should be made fun of or humiliated for his or her
> communication style.
>
> Encourage the other siblings to wait if an intro-
> verted child takes longer to give his or her opinion.
> "Heather needs a minute to think about that, Jon. Let's
> see what she thinks." By respecting everyone in the fam-
> ily, all of your children will develop stronger interper-
> sonal skills.[6]

I've had parents ask if there's any way to change their child
from an extrovert to an introvert or vice versa. No. Definitely
not. It's the way the child was created. Current research on the
brain has explained some of the reasons for these differences,
and it's pretty amazing. Brain scans and testing showed that
introverts had *more* blood flow to their brains than extroverts,
which *indicates more internal stimulation.*

Researchers also discovered that introverts' and extroverts'
blood traveled along different pathways. The introvert's pathway is more complicated and focused internally. It is a long and
complex pathway involving internal experiences such as remembering and solving problems. The extrovert's blood flow is short-
er, less complicated and travels to different areas. Extroverts
respond more to what occurs externally.[7]

MORE DIFFERENCES IN PERSONALITY

Children vary in other ways in their personality. Let's look at some of these characteristics, and how to communicate with them:

- Some children are very factual in their thinking. Give them facts rather than feelings when you talk to them.

- Some children are very brief and to the point. They are called condensers. They will listen to you if you condense (a couple of sentences), but if you are an expander and you expand (more than a couple of sentences), you will lose their attention. Additionally, if you ramble rather than sticking to the point, these children may get impatient.

- Some children stay calm and objective when others are upset. If you approach them from an emotional perspective, connecting with them is difficult.

- Some children are very truth oriented in their communication. If you want to get their attention, be sure to give the truth and nothing but the truth.

If you have a son or daughter who reflects some of these characteristics, you could at some point in time share with him or her the following:

I like the way you are so logical and factual. You've really developed that side of your life. I wonder if you've ever considered developing the other side of your life as well. There are many good benefits from knowing how to express your feelings to others.

First, feelings are actually a source of energy. When

you are aware of how you feel about something, it can actually motivate you to do a better job. Sometimes when you are thinking about something, you may want to stop and ask yourself how you feel about it.

Second, when you share your feelings either in person or on paper, it helps to get rid of stress and tension in your life.

Third, some kids respond more to feelings than to facts. If you share your feelings, they will listen to you more often, like you better and be willing to consider what you suggest to them.

Fourth, when you are disappointed and hurt, you'll actually feel better if you admit your inner pain and talk it over with someone. Burying your feelings is like burying a lighted stick of dynamite inside you. Some day it may explode when you least expect it.

Finally, believe it or not, many of the people you know like to talk about feelings. If you learn to talk about your feelings with them, they will respond to you more positively.

Yet other children live on their feelings and look at life subjectively. Some children are very concerned about people liking them. They need an abundance of verbal affirmation, which includes "feeling" words.

If you have a daughter or son who reflects some of these characteristics and shares his or her feelings with you, don't respond with a lot of facts. First, communicate to the level of his or her feelings. For example, if your child says, "I'm worried about the spelling test tomorrow," don't jump in with, "Give me your list of words and I'll start quizzing you." He or she may need your help eventually, but respond first with a statement such as, "Thinking about your spelling test has upset you. I can see your concern in your eyes. It will sure be wonderful when the test is over, won't it?" Once you've connected with your child in his or her language, your child may be open to practicing the spelling words with you.

To motivate this child, share both the task you want the child to accomplish and your feelings about his or her compliance. One mother said, "I used to make a list of specific tasks I wanted my daughter to do, and sometimes I would give reasons. But it didn't seem to work. So I started telling her how I would feel about her doing it as well as how she might feel about herself for completing the jobs. What a difference!" Keep in mind that this child usually is very sensitive to criticism.

Another personality characteristic difference is that some children are extremely literal. They want specific answers to specific questions. For example, if a child asks you the time, he or she wants it to the exact minute. When you talk with the child, don't share generalities, go around the barn a few times or change the subject in the middle of a sentence. With some children you can do this if it is their communication style, but with an extremely literal child you cannot.

If you want to get this child's attention, be factual and direct. Let the child know exactly what you are talking about as soon as you start talking. The child prefers to communicate like an article reads on the front page of a newspaper. The first sentence provides a factual summary in capsule form, while the next three paragraphs go into greater detail. Don't ask the child to analyze or solve a problem—and don't share your feelings about it—before you give him or her a concrete description. The child wants the bottom line first.

There are many other characteristics of children, but I think you are getting the idea. Study your child's thinking and talking.

Compare your styles. Then make the necessary adjustments to communicate to your child in his or her style. Your child will listen!

CHAPTER 2

Listening, Timing and Connecting

"Listen?! His eyes glaze over," a parent said. "He doesn't know the meaning of the word."

How do you get kids and teens to listen to you? Listen to *them*. Model what you want. You'll be amazed at what you'll learn.

One of the greatest gifts you can give your kids is the gift of listening. It is a biblical mandate. As James 1:19 tells us, we are to be ready listeners.

Listening is a gift of spiritual significance that you can learn to give to others. In Proverbs we read, "The hearing ear and the seeing eye—the Lord has made both of them" (20:12, *AMP*). When you listen to your child or teen, you give him or her a sense of importance, hope and love that your child may not receive any other way. Through listening, we nurture and validate the feelings the child has, especially when he or she experiences difficulties in life.

Anyone who answers without listening is foolish and confused (Prov. 18:13, *NCV*).

Any story sounds true until someone tells the other side and sets the record straight (Prov. 18:17, *TLB*).

The wise man learns by listening; the simpleton can learn only by seeing scorners punished (Prov. 21:11, *TLB*).

Let every man be quick to hear [a ready listener] (Jas. 1:19, *AMP*).

How do you get kids and teens to listen to you? Listen to **them.**

UNDERSTAND THE DIFFERENCE BETWEEN LISTENING AND HEARING

What does listening mean to you? What does hearing mean to you? Is there a difference? Hearing involves gaining content or information for your *own* purposes. Listening involves caring for and being empathetic toward your *child*. Hearing means that you are concerned about what is going on inside *you* during the conversation. And yes, sometimes you do want just the information. Real listening is difficult. It means that you are trying to understand the feelings of your child or teen and are listening for his or her sake. That's a big difference, and often children can tell the difference!

This is what real listening means: Listening means that you're not thinking about what you're going to say when your son or daughter stops talking. You're not busy formulating your response. (Ever done that? Who hasn't?) You're concentrating on what is being said and you're putting into practice Proverbs 18:13 (NCV): "Anyone who answers without listening is foolish and confused."

Listening means that you're completely accepting of what is said, without judging what your child or teen says or how he or she says it. This is not always easy, especially when your child or teen uses a negative tone of voice. If you don't like your child's choice of words or his or her tone of voice—and your child does use tones that push your buttons—and you react on the spot, you may miss the meaning! Perhaps your child hasn't spoken in the best way, but do you always speak perfectly? We all sometimes wish we could push rewind and take our words back. Why not listen and then come back later to discuss the proper wording and tone of voice? You could say, "I'd like to talk about your tone and use of words in our last interchange. Here's what and how I wish I had responded." Your child will take his or her cue from you. Acceptance doesn't mean that you agree with the content of what is said; it means that you acknowledge and understand that what is said is something your child feels.

Finally, listening means being able to repeat what your child or teen said and express what you think he or she felt while speaking to you. Real listening implies having an interest in your child's feelings and opinions, and attempting to understand those feelings from his or her perspective. When you can do that, you've started to communicate.

Hear and See

Listening is a learnable skill—for you and your child. Your mind and ears can be taught to hear more keenly; your eyes can be taught to see more clearly. You can also learn to *hear* with your eyes and *see* with your ears. Jesus said:

Therefore I speak to them in parables; because while see-ing they do not see, and while hearing they do not hear, nor do they understand. In their case the prophecy of Isaiah is being fulfilled, which says, "You will keep on hearing, but will not understand; you will keep on seeing, but will not perceive; for the heart of this people has become dull, with their ears they scarcely hear, and they have closed their eyes, otherwise they would see with their eyes, hear with their ears, and understand with their heart and return, and I would heal them" (Matt. 13:13-15).

This happens all the time in the family. Therefore, as a parent, let your ears hear and see and let your eyes see and hear.

Practice Caring Listening

There are many types of listening. Some parents listen for facts, information and details for their own use. Other parents listen because they feel sorry for their kids. Some people listen to gos-sip, because they just love a juicy story when someone else mess-es up. Other people listen out of obligation or necessity, or to be polite. Some people who listen are nothing more than voyeurs who have an incessant need to pry and probe into other people's lives. Yet some people listen because they care. And that is a par-ent's calling.

Why do we listen to our children? The five basic reasons why we listen to our children:

1. To understand our children or teens
2. To enjoy them
3. To learn something from them
4. To give help, assistance or comfort to them
5. Because we love our children

In order for caring listening to happen, we need to be aware of some of the common obstacles to communication.

Defensiveness is one. Mom or Dad, do you know what the word "defensiveness" means? Most people do. And when defensiveness happens, you miss the message because your mind is too busy thinking up a rebuttal, excuse or exception to what your children are saying. Parents want to correct their children. They want them to know they've got the last word.

There are a variety of defensive responses. *Perhaps you reach a premature conclusion*: "All right, I know just what you're going to say. We've been through this before and it's the same old thing." You might cut your children off in midsentence. Perhaps you *think* you know what they're going to say. Instead, sit back, relax and say, "I'd like to hear what you have to say."

You may read into your children's words your own expectations or even project onto them what you would say in the same situation. This is not true listening. Yet the following is true listening:

Listening is giving sharp attention to what your child *shares* with you. It's more than just hearing what he or she *says*. Often what your child *shares* is more than what he or she *says*. (Read that sentence again. It's a key thought.) You must listen to the total person, not just the words spoken. Listening requires an openness to whatever is being shared: feelings, attitudes or concerns, as well as words. It means you hear the way it's packaged. Listening also means putting yourself in a position to respond to what your child says. You may want to think about it for a while before you respond. And often that's the best thing to do. Watch your responses. When you don't like what you're hearing, your body will show it. Stay relaxed. Loosen your shoulders, unfurl your brow, unfold your arms, don't tap your foot, slow your pace of talking, watch your tone and face your child.

It is important that you listen carefully to what your child or teen says, and even more carefully to the message behind his or her words. Treat every opportunity to spend time with your child as a unique gift from God—a gift that you'll never experience in exactly the same way again. And allow the time you spend with your child to be a gift from him or her to you.

Treat every opportunity to spend time with your child as a unique gift from God. And allow the time you spend with your child to be a gift from him or her to you.

If your child drops a major bomb on you when you're in the middle of something important, give an estimate of how long you'll be, tell your child you want to hear him or her with your full, undivided attention and ask for your child's patience. Then stop at the time you told your child you would, and thank your child for bringing up what he or she said: "Wow, I'd love to hear what you wanted to say. Would you like me to just listen or would you like me to give some suggestions?"

Listening is an expression of love. It involves caring enough to take seriously what your child is communicating.

When your child knows you hear him or her, your child will trust you and feel safe with you. And if you're a good listener, your child will be more apt to invite you into his or her life. Your child also learns through your example to respond openly and lovingly to what *you* share with him or her.

Remember that there is a difference between listening and

hearing. Earlier we said the goal of hearing is to gain content or information for your *own* purposes. In hearing, you are concerned about what is going on inside *you* during the conversation. You are tuned in to your *own* responses, thoughts and feelings.

But with your child, you want to be a listener. You want to care for and empathize with your child. In listening, you want to try to understand your child's thoughts and feelings. You are listening for your child's sake, not your own.

Keep this thought in mind. When your child or teen talks to you hoping that you will listen, what is your child's purpose? Your child is either telling you something about who he or she is or about his or her life, or perhaps your child wants something. Next time your child shares with you and then pauses, what will you say? You could validate your child, make a suggestion, take action or say, "Tell me some more." "What do you think would be best?" or "Let me think about that." Delaying your response to think it through is often a wise response.

Ultimately, good listening starts with silence. When your child does something wrong, the more you listen to your child, the more information you'll have to respond back to. Sometimes it's difficult as a parent to keep quiet. You have so much to say that your children need to hear. But remember, the younger the child, the less likely what your child shares needs a comment from you. It's easy for you to put thoughts into words, but it can be a laborious experience for a pre-schooler. Don't fill in your child's words or try to hurry your child along.

When your child shares a problem or a critical concern with you, don't immediately give advice. Learn to use questions. You'll end up learning so much more. The following are a few questions you could use when communicating with your child:

- What was going on in your mind when you did that?
- Have you thought of what else you could have done?
- Did you hope things would turn out this way or . . . ?
- What do you think you could do to make things better?
- What do you think could be done to resolve this?
- If you were me what would you do now?[1]

COMMUNICATE BY TOUCHING AND LOOKING

There is another effective way to communicate: without words. We say so much without ever using words. Touching and hugging convey more than can be said with any words. Our retarded son, Matthew, was only 18 months old mentally when he died at the age of 22. We touched him affectionately and hugged him a lot, but for years he never hugged back. It was a one-sided display of affection. When he was about 15, something happened in his development and training. Once or twice a year he would reach out with his arms and put them around us when we gave him a hug. In one way it wasn't a lot, yet in another way it meant the world to us. Don't go without touching in your home.

You can also connect with your child with your eyes. Look your child in the eyes when you talk with him or her. Even a wink tells your child, "I love you." Your eyes convey the silent language of love.

PICK YOUR TIME TO COMMUNICATE

In Proverbs 15:23 (*AMP*) we read, "A word spoken at the right moment—how good it is!" *When* you talk with your child is just as important as *how* you talk with your child. When is the best time of day to talk with your child or teen? There are prime times for every family including in the morning, after school, mealtime, bedtime and Band-Aid time.

In the Morning

What do you talk about in the morning? Are your first words a positive, pleasant greeting or a grumpy, task-oriented set of orders? What occurs at this time can set the tone for the rest of the day. You can easily to fall into the trap of barking orders: "You forgot your books." "You're going to be late *again*." "Do I have to tell you again?" "Eat your breakfast. You have to have energy." Some alternative comments include "I saw your books on the piano. You might want to put them by the front door now," "Let's both watch the clock, then neither of us will be late today," and "I read the weather report and it's going to be cold. I'm wearing my warm jacket, are you wearing yours?"

After School

What occurs during the first four minutes at the end of the school day between you and your child can set the tone for the next few hours. You may feel that your child has little to say because of his or her initial response to your questions. As one parent complained, "I ask, 'How was your day?' and all I get is 'Okay' or 'Fine.' Then I ask, 'What did you do?' and I get 'stuff.'" Actually, this child did answer the questions. Perhaps your child needs downtime to recoup before you get the whole story. And perhaps you could rephrase some of your questions. You could make observations rather than grilling your child: "You look tired today." "You look like you had a bright day." "You look a bit discouraged." "Was this one of your better days or one of your bummer days?" And, of course, physical contact is a must![2]

At Mealtime

Mealtime can be hectic or delightful. You may have to work at making this a positive time. One parent said, "We had to work at having our dinner together four to five nights a week. There is no TV on, no video games at the table, no beepers. The phone is off the hook or all ringers are off, and no one leaves early. We talk and sometimes each person shares what is important to him or her today. Other times questions are taped to the bottom of the plate and each person can ask another person the question on that piece of paper. We also have a rule that when someone is talking no one can interrupt him or her."

Another family had a tradition with their three sons. Once a month they had a roundtable discussion at breakfast. Each person had five minutes to tell what was going on in his or her life and how he or she felt about it without interruption. If the person needed another five minutes, he or she could have it. It was the individual's own personal time.

At Bedtime

Bedtime is an occasion when a child can unwind and may be prompted to share things he or she wouldn't share during the day. In fact, many times a child says more than he or she wants in order to stall bedtime for another 10 minutes. Some parents sit with their child and ask, "What were the good times of today? What were the bad times?"

At Band-Aid Time

You're probably wondering what Band-Aid time is. It's when your child comes to you with either a physical or emotional ouch. How you respond at such a crucial time can reinforce independence or dependence in your child. How do you respond when your eight-year-old child trips while skating, falls down and skins his or her knee? Here are four possibilities:

1. "Oh, you poor thing. You hurt your little knee. Now, you come into the house, lie down and let Mommy fix it for you. You rest a while and I'll bring you your favorite snack." (This response teaches the child how to get attention and great treatment.)
2. "You're so clumsy. I told you you're too young to try that. Get into the house and put your skates away. We'll wait until you've got better balance. Listen to me next time." (This response is a good way to make the child feel inadequate.)
3. "Oh, don't worry, honey. It wasn't your fault. Those aren't the best skates. And that stupid sidewalk has all those cracks and bumps in it. The city needs to fix things like that so that you don't trip." (This response teaches the child to blame whatever is handy. The child is not learning to take responsibility.)
4. "John, it's just a scratch. I'll put a bandage on it now and we'll clean it up later when you take a bath. Go back and skate some more. Everyone falls down when they're learning. I know I did. I had a sore bottom for days one time. You're doing good and pretty soon you won't be falling down." (This response is realistic and teaches the child to keep the event in perspective. This is a supportive teaching response.)[3]

Yet another time for quality conversations is when driving. Often this can turn into a time of correction or advice. It helps when all handheld games are off, as well as the radio and all headsets.[4]

GIVE YOUR CHILD A TIME TO SHARE

Communication includes many elements. It involves talking, but it also includes silence, as previously mentioned. Often what isn't said can be the most significant interaction between parent and child. Have you ever considered what might be left unsaid between you and your child? Perhaps as a parent you feel that you can and have said anything you want. But what about your child? Can your child tell you everything? Does your child feel as though he or she has permission to share? Do you show as much interest in your child as a person as you do in your child's activities, or in what your child has created or accomplished?

Often what isn't said can be the most significant interaction between parent and child.

The authors of *What Did I Just Say!?!* have suggested that every parent and child need five minutes a day of genuine, intense communication. You may think that's not very much time, and you already give that much. But do you? The problem is, most of us communicate on the run, doing two or three things simultaneously. Can you think of the last time you and your child sat down and talked face-to-face—no TV, no computer, no games, no food—just the two of you eyeball-to-eyeball? Many parents have difficulty remembering times like these.

Here's what you can do:

1. Spend five minutes a day alone, away from everyone else and all interruptions, with every child in your

family, every single day. Don't allow any other activities to go on. During this time, your child gets to talk to you about anything he or she would like to talk about. You are to listen—don't talk, don't interpret, don't interrupt and don't correct your child's version. Your job is to listen, understand and validate how your child *feels* about what he or she says. Why do this? It costs nothing, takes little time, connects you to your child on a regular basis, builds a calming effect, promotes open, honest sharing and draws the two of you closer together.

2. Start this habit by letting your child know that you are going to begin a special time for the two of you each day. Let your child know that he or she can say whatever he or she thinks and feels, and you'll be there to listen. You may get some resistance or smart remarks about this time. That's all right. Don't get hooked into a battle. Just do it.

3. Follow the rules. Private time means this time belongs only to your child. Bathroom, phone, pager, other kids, spouse, dog—none of these can distract you. Remember, this needs to be done one-on-one. Both parents need their own time with each child. It is possible. A friend of mine gave one hour of private time to each of his five children each week for years. It did wonders for his family.

4. The five minutes spent in private time *each day* is essential. If you have to miss, pick it up the next day. If you are detained, it can be done over the phone. But the same rules apply—the child shares what he or she wants. Avoid factual reports of games and outings; instead, ask your child how he or she feels.

Remember, this is not a democratic process. Just because the child gets five minutes, doesn't mean the parent gets five minutes. Your child needs to be understood and accepted. If your child wants to sit silently for five minutes, that's all right. Don't interrupt what your child thinks. Your child could be talking to you in his or her mind. Some children might take days or weeks to open up; therefore, don't just fill the silence with words. This is the time for your child to share whatever has been building inside. Your child needs to do it respectfully, though.[5]

BE POSITIVE AND APPRECIATIVE

Some parents seem to be on a mission: They feel called to catch their child doing something wrong, disobeying or failing to follow through. What a parent looks for, he or she will find. These are parents who usually jump all over their children for their discovered mistakes. Unfortunately, this usually reinforces the child's behavior, which causes a recurring effect.

I have two golden retrievers. They are wonderful family dogs. I've invested time and attention in both their care and their training. Shadow is a puppy in training to be a therapy dog. Aspen goes out and retrieves the paper. We will drop or throw an item to be discarded on the floor and say, "Trash," and Aspen will pick it up and take it to the trash can. I can place Aspen at my side without a leash and walk a half-mile with her right next to my left side. A few times I will say, "Heel," and she obeys, because that's what she's been trained to do. A previous dog I had, Sheffield, would pick up the phone and bring it to me. These aren't superdogs; they were just trained. How? In their training when they didn't do something right, nothing was said. Instead, we just tried it again. When the dogs did something right, they heard about it big time. They received verbal praise, a touch, a tummy rub or a pat on the head.

People are no different. When your child does something right, let him or her hear about it. When your child messes up, don't reinforce it. Instead, focus on what your child *will* do differently next time.

All of us need to be recognized for who we are and what we have done. Appreciation imparts a feeling of significance.

When you give corrective requests, make them positive rather than negative. It's easy to tell a child what to stop doing. It's second nature for some of us. Have you found yourself making statements like "I want you to stop being rough to the cat." "I want you to stop talking." or "I want you to stop arguing with me"?

If not these statements, I'm sure you have your own list of "I want you to stop . . . " statements. Again, the emphasis here is on what is negative—what you don't want to happen. To be positive, simply change your request to what you want your child to do: "I want you to be gentle and kind to your cat," "I want you to be quiet now," or "I want you to do what I say and stop playing Nintendo now."

A parent asked me, "Norm, I've changed my requests like this, but sometimes I get an argument. I get resistance or noncompliance. She wants to keep playing on the computer and tells me she doesn't want to stop." What could this parent say? What would you say at this time? You could acknowledge your child's desire not to stop by saying, "I understand you want to keep playing, but I want you to come get ready for church." After that, no matter what response you get back from your child, just say in a calm, soft voice, "I want you to come now and get ready for church." Learn to express what *you* want instead of reinforcing what your *child* wants to keep doing. And you don't always have to give reasons.

CHAPTER 3

When You Talk, Nurture

One of our goals as parents should be to enable our children to think as highly of themselves as God thinks of them. A chief means for accomplishing this goal is to convey nurturing messages, both verbally and nonverbally. If you fill their lives with positive messages of their value to you and to God, they will develop self-worth and self-discipline, and become responsible, independent adults. Ideally, parent-child communication is filled with nurturing messages.

Nurturing messages convey to your children something good about themselves. These positive messages don't increase your children's value, because your children are already priceless in God's eyes. However, nurturing messages increase your children's value in *their own eyes*, thus opening the door for learning, growth, maturity and independence.

Parents need to nurture their children every day. Casual, spontaneous comments and planned, direct eye-to-eye statements are equally effective. Nurturing involves giving more affirmations than corrections. Keep a written account of your messages to your child for a few days to see to which side the scale is tipped. If you make a point to share nurturing messages every day, it will soon become an automatic response.

By the way, do you nurture yourself? Have you ever thought about yourself as a work of art? You are. So is each child. The sculptor, our Lord and Savior, has been chipping away at you for some time and will continue to do so. Consider this:

When a fanatic dealt several damaging blows to Michelangelo's Pieta, the world was horrified. It surprised no one when the world's best artists assembled to refashion the disfigured masterpiece.

Your children are already priceless in God's eyes. However, nurturing messages increase your children's value in their own eyes.

When the sculptors arrived in Italy, they didn't begin repairing the marred face immediately. Rather they spent months looking at the Pieta, touching the flowing lines, appreciating the way each part expressed suffering yet ecstasy. Some spent months studying a single part such as the hand until finally the sculptors began to see more and more with the eyes of Michelangelo and to touch and feel as the master artist would have done. When the sculptors finally began repairing the face, the strokes belonged almost as much to Michelangelo as to themselves.

Not Michelangelo's but rather God's sculpturing hand fashioned us from soil-dust into a masterpiece which surpassed even the Pieta (see Gen. 2:7). It would not surprise us that God constantly refashions us—that as soon as we disfigure ourselves, He's already sculpturing the pieces back together.[1]

Sometimes we disfigure ourselves by what we think about ourselves rather than by what we do to ourselves. It is difficult to nurture our children if we don't nurture ourselves. Some people have been disfigured emotionally because of what others did to them when they were children. Sometimes our memory banks becomes warehouses of beliefs and feelings that cripple our progress.

In a sense, you're also a sculptor fashioning your child. The words and looks you use are the tools that leave imprints. The younger the child, the more he or she resembles moldable clay rather than hard granite. Nurturing words shape the heart. As you allow the Holy Spirit to rework and refashion your beliefs about yourself, drawing you closer to Christ's image, your skills as a potter or sculptor will be refined.

HOW TO CONVEY NURTURING MESSAGES

Nurturing shows that you believe in your child's capacity to learn, change and grow. Nurturing shows that you are aware of the kind of picture you want your child to have of himself or herself. Your child's mind is like a computer. Every message you send your child goes into one of two files: discounting or nurturing. The file with the most data will direct how your child sees and feels about himself or herself. When nurturing occurs on a regular basis, victim blame cannot gain a foothold in your child's life.

Messages that nurture are based on unconditional love, which must be worked at, especially if you come from a discounting family. You will need to rely on Jesus Christ to fill the void in your life with His presence and help you learn how to love unconditionally like He loves us.

Let's look at two types of nurturing messages that will help develop healthy, self-disciplined children: (1) affirmation and compliments for good behavior and right choices; and (2) nurturing messages of correction for bad behavior and wrong choices.

Affirmation and Compliments for Good Behavior and Right Choices

It is easier for most parents to affirm positive behavior than to deal with negative behavior in a positive way. We must continually remind ourselves to convey nurturing affirmations and compliments such as the following:

- "You treat your friends very nicely."
- "You have a wonderful ability with tools."
- "Thanks for doing such a good job on your chores today."
- "Your schoolwork has really improved."
- "I liked the way you cleaned your room. Thank you."
- "You're a very special person to me."
- "I'm so glad you're my child."
- "I love you because you deserve to be loved. You don't have to earn it."
- "You make my life more complete just by being you."
- "I'm glad I have you. You teach me so much about life."

Such affirmations cause children to realize, *Mom and Dad really love me. They think I'm a lovable person. My needs are important to them. They want to help me face the problems of life and solve them. What happens to me is very important to them. They trust me to think for myself and make good decisions.*

As you convey nurturing messages, be sure your value judgments are attached to your child's behavior, not your child's personality. For example, a toddler exploring the family room approaches the television, which is within the toddler's reach. Fascinated by the shiny knobs and switches, the toddler reaches out to touch the TV. The toddler's mother says, "Don't touch, Joshua. Remember, I said you can look at the television, but you can't touch it. Here are some other things you can touch." She jiggles a box of toys. Joshua stands in front of the TV for a moment, wrestling with the temptation. Then he turns away from the TV toward the toys.

What would you say to affirm Joshua? Many of us would remark, "Good boy, Joshua!" However, if Joshua had touched the TV against his mother's wishes, many of us would remark, "Bad boy, Joshua!" Do you notice why those kinds of statements are value judgments on Joshua? He soon learns that he is sometimes good and sometimes bad, which confuses his self-perception.

Instead, Joshua's mother should say, "Good *choice*, Joshua!" She wants him to learn that he is capable of making good choices, for which he is affirmed, and bad choices, for which he is corrected. Despite the choice Joshua makes, he should always be regarded and nurtured as a good boy. This subtle but important distinction can make a world of difference in your child's self-image.

Nurturing Messages of Correction for
Bad Behavior and Wrong Choices

When our children make wrong choices or misbehave, they need to be corrected. But since we are concerned with nurturing them at all times, corrective messages must be delivered in a positive, affirmative way. We don't correct our children to make them feel bad but to help them discover a better way to do something. Here are a few examples of nurturing statements of correction:

- "Here is a way you can do it that you might like better."
- "It sounds like it's hard for you to accept a compliment. Perhaps you need more practice accepting them, and I need more practice giving them."
- "I'm not sure you heard what I said. Tell me what you heard, and then let me repeat what I said if you heard differently."
- "You can't do that any longer, but you can do this instead."
- "That was a poor choice you made, but I have some good ideas you may want to consider for getting back on track."
- "You're not paying attention. Something must be on your mind, since you are so good at listening and thinking. I wonder what it is?"

Whenever you need to tell your child, "Stop it," be sure to include in your message what your child may do instead. If you don't add some positive suggestions, your correction will be interpreted as negative criticism. It may stop your child from engaging in a hurtful or destructive activity, but it fails to build your child's self-discipline and confidence in an alternative area.

Share your messages of correction in a tone of voice that reflects your care and concern. Your tone has five times the impact as your words. Also, convey corrective messages with an affirmative touch on the hand or shoulder, or with a hug. Your nonverbal affirmations will convey your love and care even in an uncomfortable confrontation.

As you learn to nurture your child through positive verbal

and nonverbal messages, your child will feel comforted, loved and helped. To be most effective, your nurturing messages must be freely given and specifically tailored to meet the unique needs of your child. Each comment must be appropriate to the child and to the setting—not overdone or underdone.

Your tone has five times the impact as your words.

What's the payoff? Your nurturing efforts will promote maturity and independence in your child by helping your child think and do for himself or herself. As you nurture your child through adulthood, you will have the satisfaction of knowing that you helped your child succeed at caring for himself or herself.[2]

Scriptures of Truth for Healthy Communication

What is the best resource to follow for knowing how to communicate? It is the Scriptures. The Word of God is the most effective resource for learning to communicate. In it you will find a workable pattern for healthy relationships. Here are just a few of the guidelines the Bible offers:

> But speaking the truth in love, we are to grow up in all aspects into Him who is the head, even Christ (Eph. 4:15).

> A man who refuses to admit his mistakes can never be successful. But if he confesses and forsakes them, he gets another chance (Prov. 28:13, *TLB*).

For we all stumble in many ways. If anyone does not stumble in what he says, he is a perfect man, able to bridle the whole body as well (Jas. 3:2).

Let him who wants to enjoy life and see good days [good—whether apparent or not] keep his tongue from evil and his lips from guile (1 Pet. 3:10, *AMP*).

Some people like to make cutting remarks, but the words of the wise soothe and heal (Prov. 12:18, *TLB*).

A wise man controls his temper. He knows that anger causes mistakes (Prov. 14:29, *TLB*).

Gentle words cause life and health; griping brings discouragement. . . . Everyone enjoys giving good advice, and how wonderful it is to be able to say the right thing at the right time! (Prov. 15:4,23, *TLB*).

Timely advice is as lovely as golden apples in a silver basket (Prov. 25:11, *TLB*).

A friendly discussion is as stimulating as the sparks that fly when iron strikes iron (Prov. 27:17, *TLB*).

Pride leads to arguments; be humble, take advice and become wise (Prov. 13:10, *TLB*).

Love forgets mistakes; nagging about them parts the best of friends (Prov. 17:9, *TLB*).

Let all bitterness and wrath and anger and clamor and

slander be put away from you, along with all malice. Be kind to one another, tenderhearted, forgiving each other, just as God in Christ also has forgiven you (Eph. 4:31-32).

Why not go back to each Scripture and summarize each principle? What a difference it would make if each family member followed these guidelines.

How to Use Encouraging Words

Sometimes talking positively to your child when he or she acts out is difficult. When your child acts out, he or she often needs some encouraging words.

How can you encourage someone with an obvious problem behavior? Is it possible to still speak kindly to someone who isn't responding well? Does your child have some type of behavior that you would like to corral like a herd of wild horses? Asking the last question to a group of parents usually leads to some interesting responses:

- "I wish we could control the griping and complaining that goes on in our family."
- "What I don't like are the sarcastic put-down comments that all of us make."
- "Blame. That's what gets to me. Blame, blame, blame. Nobody admits to their part in a problem, they just point the finger at others."

Did you hear these responses? They are all communication problems. Here's what you can do to improve your family's communication.

You first need to identify and confine a negative behavior that you would like to eliminate from your family's interaction. Then ask each family member when and where the negative behavior usually occurs (i.e., what time of day and in which room of the house). Is it done when people are sitting down or standing up, far from one another or close together? Is the television off or on? Does it continue if the phone rings or if someone visits? Who is best (or worst) at this particular behavior?

After you have gathered the needed information, suggest a new approach. Here is what one father said to his family:

> I've noticed that we have a number of complaints that we like to make and get off our chest. That's understandable since all of us have things that we would like to see changed from time to time. But we need a better way to deal with our complaints, so we will begin to have a family complaint time. The only time this will occur is Tuesday and Thursday nights from 7:15 to 7:30. It will be held in the den. This will be our complaint time and complaint room.
>
> We cannot make complaints at any other time, so I suggest that you write them down in order to remember them. We are not to complain to anyone at any other time. When you do have a complaint to share, we will all listen to you. We will not interrupt you or defend ourselves. We will consider your complaint. However, when you share your complaint, you also need to come up with a positive solution or suggestion that you would like us to consider.[3]

During the first two weeks of this family's complaint time, a number of complaints slipped out of various family members.

For each slip, they were told, "Write it down and save it for the meeting." After a while they remembered and the dinner times especially became more enjoyable and livable.[4]

When complaints are in the form of sarcasm or put-downs, it may be helpful to explore hurt feelings. Healthier ways of expressing anger could be suggested, as well as more constructive ways of responding to family members.

When families resolve problems, everyone feels encouraged by the progress. And encouraged families tend to be more creative in their shared activities. What have you done recently to generate new life in your family? The routine rut can so easily creep into our busy lives. We soon become captive to regular patterns, schedules, discussions, entertainment and activities, resulting in the hurry-up-and-rush-through-life syndrome. "Frantic" is the word that best describes the way many of us live our lives. This is how one father described the atmosphere of his family: "Everyone seems to be on this schedule where we've always got too much to do. We all collapse at the end of the day. It's at the point where we don't enjoy anything or anyone anymore! That's not the way it should be!"

How is your family life? Does it feel hectic, driven, in a rut? What can you do to make your family life more fulfilling and encouraging? Here is one family's approach:

The Wilson family consisted of two parents and five children, ranging in ages from 7 to 16. One of their unique rules had a profound effect upon the family. When anyone arrived home at the end of the day—whether from school or work—everyone was to be greeted in a positive way. No griping or negative comments could be shared right away. They would show interest and concern to each one, as well as share hugs and kisses. The Wilsons believed that what occurred during the first four minutes set the tone for the rest of the evening. If the initial interactions were negative and critical, the remainder of the evening would follow suit. On the other hand, a positive start usually lasted throughout the evening.

When Dad arrived home, no requests from the children were allowed. In times past, he was frequently inundated by verbal requests as soon as he came through the door. After greeting the children, he and his wife would spend the next 15 minutes alone in the kitchen without any interference or interruptions from the children. Naturally this elicited a number of comments from the kids, but they learned to respect their parents' privacy. After dinner, the children shared their requests in writing, which gave their parents a chance to consider them without pleas, arguments and time pressure.

Unrealistic? This approach won't work? Not true at all. Creative families will make an approach like this work.

HERE COMES THE JUDGE

Have you ever found yourself judging your child? Parents speak judgmentally for the purpose of controlling their children. However, the usual results are discouragement, dejection and reinforcement of the characteristic the parents actually want to change. When you fire the guns of judgment, your child ends up overloaded with blame, which makes your child feel unacceptable to you and to himself or herself. There are several traps of judgement we can fall into.

Belittlement

Belittling is one of the most damaging forms of judgment. Your child is belittled when you make light of his or her behavior, feelings, thoughts or accomplishments. Any kind of belittling conveys to your child that his or her feelings, ideas or behavior are no good. The bottom line of this message is an emotional time bomb: You are no good.

Your child will respond to belittlement by withdrawing from you in a number of ways. Your child may not listen to you, clam up or not share anything of substance with you. Or your child may strike back in some less obvious way. Therefore, communication problems are perpetuated.

Blame

Blaming is another toxic verbal weapon of judgment. I've seen parents use this approach to avoid accepting responsibility for their own actions. They blame their children for "causing" their problems or emotional upsets. You've probably heard yourself or other parents say to a child:

- "You make me so upset."
- "Your behavior is going to be the death of me."
- "I wish you wouldn't make me so angry."

What they are actually saying is, "This wouldn't have happened if it hadn't been for you. You're responsible!" How can a child—who is less able to understand life and relationships than an adult—handle such a statement of blame? And did you hear the "you" messages?

Sometimes a parent blames a child for something the child did well but could have done better. The following statements are examples of how a parent can hammer a child with the words "should" and "shouldn't":

- "You should have done it my way."
- "You should have been done sooner."
- "You shouldn't have worn your good clothes outside."
- "You shouldn't ever do that in this home."

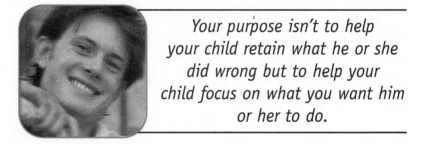

Your purpose isn't to help your child retain what he or she did wrong but to help your child focus on what you want him or her to do.

What the parent is pointing out to the child may be valid, but "should" is often a weapon of blame, which wounds the child and can reinforce the very behavior or attitude the parent is attempting to correct. A child translates "you should have" as "you did it wrong." Your purpose isn't to help your child retain what he or she did wrong but to help your child focus on what you want him or her to do. Therefore, instead of using "should" and "shouldn't," phrase your statement in a way that leaves a positive impression: "I appreciate what you did. Here's another way you might want to try next time." When you nurture in this way, your child will listen.

A book that I highly recommend to help you in the nurturing process is Dr. Tim Kimmel's *Grace-Based Parenting* (W Publishing Group, 2004).[5]

CHAPTER 4

Communication Basics

"How's your attitude?"

"My what?"

"Your attitude, especially toward your children. I find that some parents want to just talk about the problems they have with their children or teens."

Most parents have a laundry list of problem behaviors. What's interesting is no one usually asks them what is wrong with their children or teens. Yet what's wrong is usually on the forefront of their minds. What about you? What's your focus?

If I asked you, "What does your child do right? What are your child's positive behaviors?" what would you say? Most of the time a child's positive behavior far exceeds his or her negative behavior, but we tend to concentrate on what is not working rather than what is working.

ACKNOWLEDGE AND REINFORCE POSITIVE BEHAVIOR

Let me turn to sports for a minute. I enjoy baseball. Sometimes even the best hitters fall into a hitting slump, and they try and try to break out of it. They consult with their hitting coaches and analyze what they're doing wrong, so they can get back on track. Many hitters watch videos of themselves batting to see what they can learn. Yet usually the videos they select make all the difference. Some hitters watch videos of their poor hitting performances. They focus on their wrongdoings, find the problems and correct them. Unfortunately, this does not work well for most hitters. Other hitters select videos that show a hitting streak—when they were doing fantastic. They observe what worked. They soon reach their previous level again by concentrating on what worked.

Parenting works in a similar fashion. The best step any parent can take is to be like the hitters who focus on what works. This is the best way to solve problems. I'm sure there are many times when you and your child get along. Can you describe specifically what you and your child do differently when you get along? Think about it. Then identify it. Discover what works and then focus on what your child or teen does that you appreciate. Here is one mother's list of her daughter's positive and negative behaviors:

Michelle's Positive Behaviors

- Puts her clothes in the hamper
- Uses good manners at the dinner table
- Gives the dog water almost every day
- Puts the cap back on the toothpaste and puts the toothpaste away when she is finished with it
- Hangs up her towel
- Is quiet when she gets up on the weekend mornings and lets us sleep
- Shares her toys with friends
- Gives me lots of hugs and kisses
- Is a good reader

- Does well in school
- Does her homework independently
- Has a great laugh
- Can be a good listener
- Makes up with her sister when they have a disagreement
- Plays nicely with her sister from time to time
- Goes to bed when she is asked
- Behaves well when we go shopping
- Shows her love in special ways

Michelle's Negative Behaviors

- Has difficulty getting along with her sister
- Won't share her toys with her sister
- Hits her sister
- Cries when she doesn't get her way
- Sulks
- Tells me she hates me when she's angry
- Throws tantrums[1]

The bottom-line principle is to catch your child or teen doing something right and then reinforce that behavior.

The bottom-line principle is to catch your child or teen doing something right and then reinforce that behavior. When you witness the good behavior, praise your child immediately and describe what you've observed. Here is a simple way to jot down your child's positive behavior and your observation:

Your child's name _____
   Positive behavior   My observation

_____   _____
_____   _____
_____   _____
_____   _____
_____   _____
_____   _____
_____   _____

Once you acknowledge and praise your child's positive behavior, how will you reinforce it? What do you say when . . . ?

It is easy to express appreciation to or praise young children or teens when they do something noteworthy or do something they may have been lax about in the past. It is much more difficult to express appreciation or praise when something goes wrong. However, with practice, you can transform some of the most trying situations from negative to positive by using appreciation and praise. The following dialogue may seem extraordinary, but it can and does happen.

> *Tim (Looking ashen.):* Mom, something terrible has happened.
> *Mom:* What happened?
> *Tim:* I'm too afraid to tell.
> *Mom:* Are you afraid of my reaction?
> *Tim:* Yes! You're going to kill me.
> *Mom:* Tim, the only way we're going to solve this problem is by talking about it.

Tim: The problem can't be solved.

Mom: As long as you're in one piece, that's all that matters.

Tim: Okay. Here it comes: I broke a plate from your good set—the expensive one.

Mom: I really love those plates, but we can replace it.

Tim: Mom, are you sure you aren't very mad?

Mom: Timmy, I am upset, but to me a broken plate is only a broken plate. The important thing is that you came and told me what happened. I appreciate that.

Tim: I wish I hadn't broken it.[2]

Tim's mother skillfully avoided criticizing and blaming. She praised Tim's forthrightness and reacted calmly when he expected fury. She distinguished between what was important and what was not: "A broken plate is only a broken plate." She wasn't indifferent to the loss of an expensive plate, but she saw it as less significant than Tim's feelings about himself. And most important, she showed Tim her appreciation for telling her what happened.

For many of us, responding as Tim's mother did would be extremely difficult.[3] Take a moment to reflect on a difficult situation between you and your child. Then answer the following questions:

1. What is the most difficult situation between you and your child?

2. What is a positive way you could respond to this situation?

REQUEST, DON'T DEMAND

A simple principle in theory, but one we don't always follow in our conversations is request rather than command or demand. We might be amazed if we started to keep track of the number of orders we give to our children: "Do this, do that." "Put that away." "Don't leave the door open." Stop doing that." "Go comb your hair." "Come to lunch." "Don't play with your food." "Get ready for bed." "Go to bed now." "Don't stop." Ironically, we repeat orders to make sure they're carried out, but repetition weakens the response.

You can raise both the listening and compliance level of your child with one simple step—ask. Instead of ordering, "Go clean your room," ask, "Would you please go and clean your room?" The word to use is "would," not "could." "Would" says "I want you to," whereas "could" asks about competency. But no matter how you phrase it, note your tone.[4]

You can raise both the listening and compliance level of your child with one simple step—ask.

When you ask, avoid any long explanations. Keep it short. Have you ever felt your child watched too much TV or spent too much time playing video games? Probably. The following are examples of what some parents may say in situations like these and brief questions to ask instead:

"Kim, you've watched way too much TV today. That noise is getting to me. Turn it off and do something else with your time. Have you done your homework yet?"

Instead, say, "Would you please turn off the TV now and do something else?"

"John, look at this room. There are clothes all over and dirty dishes—and the smell! Why can't you clean it up? I'm not going to pick up after you. Get a shovel and start cleaning."

Instead, the following would suffice, "John, would you please clean your room? Thank you."

Here are 12 common negative expressions parents say to their children or teens. Read each one and decide if you have said this or something similar. There is a place for you to fill in when you used the expression, its result and how you could rephrase the comment.

1. "You're not listening to me."

    The last time I said this was _____

    The result was _____

    The way in which I could rephrase this is _____

    _____

    _____

2. "Quit daydreaming and pay attention to me."

    The last time I said this was _____

    The result was _____

    The way in which I could rephrase this is _____

    _____

    _____

3. "Try to remember for once will you?"

The last time I said this was _____

The result was _____

The way in which I could rephrase this is _____

_____

_____

4. "I don't know what I'm going to do with you."

The last time I said this was _____

The result was _____

The way in which I could rephrase this is _____

_____

_____

5. "There is no way you'll be able to do that."

The last time I said this was _____

The result was _____

The way in which I could rephrase this is _____

_____

_____

6. "You didn't put your books (or toys, clothes and so on) away."

The last time I said this was _____

The result was _____

The way in which I could rephrase this is _____

_____

_____

7. "Your room is a total mess; it looks like a pigpen."

The last time I said this was _____

The result was _____

The way in which I could rephrase this is _____

_____

_____

8. "Stop yelling in here. You're too loud!"

The last time I said this was _____

The result was _____

The way in which I could rephrase this is _____

_____

_____

9. "You forgot to say thank-you."

The last time I said this was _____

The result was _____

The way in which I could rephrase this is _____

_____

_____

10. "You left the door open again, and your clothes are on the floor."

The last time I said this was _____

The result was _____

The way in which I could rephrase this is _____

_____

_____

11. "Don't interrupt us when we're telling you something."

The last time I said this was _____

The result was _____

The way in which I could rephrase this is _____

_____

_____

12. Give an example of a common negative expression
you usually say: _____

_____

The last time I said this was _____

The result was _____

The way in which I could rephrase this is _____

_____

_____

USE "I" MESSAGES

Have you ever had someone point a finger at you? Probably.
When it occurs, what goes on inside of you? Some think, *Uh-
oh, what did I do? I think I'm in trouble. I'm feeling defensive and I
don't want to hear anything anyone says. I think the other person is
going to say something bad about me.* Not too many of us like people pointing their fingers at us.

Are you aware that parents often point their fingers at their
children verbally? Yes, that's right, verbally. It's when you say:
"You are a bad child," "You are disrespectful," "You did this,"
"You make me so angry," or "You're driving me wacko!" "You"

messages become a natural part of our lives, even though they blame and elicit a brick wall in a young child's or teen's life. We use "you" messages more when we're upset or angry. It's a form of attack, and we become proficient at it. However, when we use "I" messages, communication tends to continue and develop. Our children are more likely to follow the "I" message pattern.

Don't think changing will be easy—you have to learn a new language.

Here are some examples:

- "I'm upset that you left the house unlocked."
- "I'm really angry over the constant arguing. I want the two of you to figure out a new way of resolving your differences."
- "I need you to tell me when you're going to be late. When I don't hear from you, I begin to worry. Why do I worry? I'm the mother of a teen!"

Don't think changing will be easy. You have to learn a new language. Start the transition by beginning your sentences with "I." Do it again and again. Practice. It will work.

UNDERSTAND YOUR NONVERBAL COMMUNICATION

Are you aware of the effect your nonverbal communication has on your child? You use gestures, body movements and eye expressions constantly, but often your awareness of them is minimal. Frequently, your words convey a message of approval or permission, but your nonverbal expressions convey a conflicting message of disapproval. This means the listener *hears* approval but *sees* disapproval. The result is confusion. Often the listener ignores the spoken message and responds to the nonverbal message. Or if the listener responds to the words, the speaker becomes irritated and the listener wonders why the speaker is upset.

Are you aware of the effect your nonverbal communication has on your child?

Body movements provide a basis for making some reasonable assumptions but not for drawing absolute conclusions. It is important, therefore, that you do the following:

1. Become aware of the nonverbal messages you send to your child.
2. Become skillful in correctly interpreting the nonverbals that your child sends to you.
3. Develop a fluency in your nonverbal skills.
4. Bring your nonverbal communication and your spoken communication into harmony.

Nonverbal communication is similar to a code. We need to learn to decipher, modify, refine and enhance it. Tone of voice and inflection add another element to the communication process. The mixture of these elements of communication can be rather complicated.

What Do You Think?

Let's consider the possible meaning of some nonverbal or voice behaviors. Look at the following list and try to think of two or three meanings to each behavior:

1. Your child or teen nods his or her head up and down.

2. Your child turns his or her head rapidly in a certain direction.

3. Your child smiles slightly.

4. Your child's lower lip quivers slightly.

5. Your child speaks in a loud, harsh voice.

6. Your child speaks in a low, monotonous voice.

7. Your child suddenly opens his or her eyes wide.

8. Your child keeps his or her eyes lowered when speaking to you.

9. Your child speaks in a very halting or hesitant voice.

10. Your child yawns during a conversation.

11. Your child shrugs his or her shoulders.

12. Your child sits rigid and upright in a chair.

13. Your child has his or her arms folded tightly across his or her chest.

14. Your child wrings her or her hands.

15. Your child holds a chair tightly with his or her hands.

16. Your child's breathing is quite irregular.

17. Your child keeps fiddling with the collar of his or her shirt.

18. Your child slouches in a chair.

19. Your child constantly squirms.

20. Your child continuously moves his or her legs back and forth.

Some parents have discovered that most of their interaction with their children or teens is "maintenance talk," which is one directive or one command after another. They sound like efficiency experts or drill sergeants trying to remake their offspring: "Get up." "Go to bed." "Get dressed." "Drink your milk." "Don't spill." "Brush your teeth." "Use toothpaste."

Parents may realize they are constantly telling their children what to do and when to do it. Constant lecturing does not build their relationships or enhance their two-way communication. Therefore, it was imperative that they begin to learn the importance of positive communication.

CHAPTER 5

Your Child Can Change

Mom: Tommy! Tommy! Tommy! Do you hear me?

Tommy: Yeah, Mom. I heard you the first time you called me.

Mom: Well, why didn't you respond, so I didn't have to yell at you?

Tommy: You didn't have to yell. I just wanted to finish what I started.

Dad: Jennifer, how was school today?

Jennifer: Oh, okay, I guess.

Dad: Well, tell me about it.

Jennifer: Same old stuff.

Dad: Well, you must have done *something* interesting. Think for a minute.

Jennifer: Ah, I don't know. What's there to eat? I'm hungry.

Dad: Oh, you. You're so frustrating at times.

Matt: Hey, Mom, I need to go over to Jimmy's now. Remember, you said I could go. Remember?

Mom: Yes, I did, but after you clean your room.

Matt: The guys are getting there early, and I want to—

Mom: That's the trouble with you. You want to when you want to! You have chores, young man, so get to them! *(Turns, walks out and slams the door.)*

Sound familiar? Just some typical scenarios in the day in the life of a parent. Each interchange involved the communication process, but each ended in frustration. What's it like in your home? Are you connecting with your child or teen? Is your child tuning you out, overriding you, not listening to you? It happens to all of us at one time or another. But it doesn't have to last. The interaction can change. You can change. Your child can change.

STEPS TO CHANGE

The way we as parents speak and act has a major impact on how our children act and talk. You can draw them to you by encouraging and nurturing or push them away by what you say. Sometimes you can push them away, not because your words are bad or negative, but because you speak a different language from your children. In other words, you're not packaging what you say so that it connects with your children's language. To move beyond the parent-child differences, you will need to (1) believe change is possible; (2) be willing to make a course correction in the direction you're heading; and (3) integrate Scripture into your communication styles.

Perhaps you're thinking, *All right, Norm. You've made your point. But I still get frustrated with our communication at times. I want my children to hear me. I want them to respond to what I say. I want to* connect. *How do I change my communication responses so that this happens?*

Step 1: Believe Change Is Possible

By asking for help, you've taken the first step. Before you can make any changes, you must acknowledge your need to change. Congratulations—you're on your way!

Step 2: Be Willing to Make a Course Correction

The second step involves clearly identifying the communication patterns that don't work. To help you do so, I suggest that you do what I've asked numerous parents in my counseling office to do: Begin recording your conversations at home. Get an audio-cassette recorder and several blank 90-minute tapes. Turn the recorder on at mealtimes, at the onset of a family argument or at other occasions when the family is together, and let it run. After a few self-conscious moments, everyone will forget about the recorder and begin to interact normally.

After you have recorded several interactions, listen to the tapes. As you listen, focus on your own communication patterns instead of judging other family members for what they say or don't say. Write down your comments from the tapes and summarize the kinds of questions and statements you use.

Step 3: Integrate Scripture

The third step is to begin integrating the guidance of Scripture into your communication. Here's a practical way to do so:

1. Write each of the following verses about communication from Proverbs on a separate index card: 10:19; 12:18; 14:29; 16:24; 17:9; 19:11; 29:20.
2. On the back of each card, write a statement describing

how you see yourself complying with that verse. Make it specific and personal, perhaps beginning with the words, "I will . . . "

3. Carry the cards with you for the next 30 days, and read each verse and statement aloud several times a day. By the end of 30 days, you probably will have memorized most of the verses and begun to integrate their concepts into your communication.

I have discovered that it is helpful to involve your spouse or a trusted friend in this process. Tell somebody what you are doing, read to them the statements you have written and ask them to hold you accountable to follow through with the exercise.

I also suggest that you keep a personal, parent-child communication-growth diary. Write down your progress in attitudes, feelings and communication daily. Stay positive; don't keep score of the problems or defeats. Note how you change and how your child responds to your changes. Share your responses with your spouse or another trusted friend. At the end of each week, reread the entire diary from the beginning. Faithfully keep your diary for one month, and then decide if you want to continue for another month.

When your words are clear, concise, nurturing and encouraging, you will connect with your child. First Thessalonians 5:11 (NIV) states: "Therefore encourage one another and build each other up, just as in fact you are doing." A child needs his or her parents to believe in his or her potential. Believe in your child. Focus on your child's resources in order to help build his or her self-esteem, self-confidence and feelings of worth. Help your child to see how God views him or her. Become a talent scout. Help your child discover his or her uniqueness, giftedness and potential. Be a model of clear communication, and your child will follow your example.

Believe in your child.

ATTENTION GETTERS

Have you ever wondered why it's difficult to get and keep your young child's or especially your teen's attention? Think about it. We as parents may be a bit boring to our children who are raised on megastimulation. Our kids are being raised on an action-oriented, sound-bite learning style. Children today more than ever before get bored quickly, and they want novel stimulation. Because you can sound like the same old thing to your children, you're easy to tune out. Therefore, you will need to be creative and flexible, and you may need to vary your approach.

One way you can connect better is when you keep your child guessing. Keep the same rules and standards, but be unpredictable in your approach. As one child said, "I never know what my mom or dad is going to do next. I've finally figured it out, though. They say the same thing and want the same thing from me, but it's always in a different package. I hear it in a new way. If it was the same old thing, I'd throw a switch and tune 'em out."

For years I've started my seminars at either 8:29 A.M. or 8:57 A.M. The brochures and confirmation state these times. Those who read this information say, "What do you mean 8:29 A.M.? What kind of time is that? Must be a misprint." But over 90 percent of the participants are present and ready to go at the appointed time. If the time was 8:30 A.M. or 9:00 A.M., I'm sure fewer people would show up on time. It's a matter of capturing attention.

Additionally, avoid asking why. Most parents ask their children why in an upsetting situation or confrontation. Asking this question is a sure way to get a defensive response such as, "I don't know." Essentially, you're trying to get your child to give you a reason. But either the child doesn't know at that moment, or does but doesn't think you'd understand or agree.

When you try to explain why when your child is upset, he or she probably doesn't care why you're doing what you're doing. Yes, your child needs to be given reasons, but wait for a time when your child is more receptive. For example, leave your child a note later in the day, and then assume it's been read. Don't check up on your child.[1] It will only create more defensive behavior.

CONSTRUCTIVE CRITICISM

Is constructive criticism really constructive? Not really. You can't make a young child or teen better by pointing out what you think is wrong with him or her. Criticism either crushes spirit or elicits defensiveness. Constructive criticism is an interesting combination of words. "Construct" means "to build." "Criticism" means "to tear down." It creates defiance and anger as well.

When I was a child, I had some difficulty with certain school subjects. They were just plain hard for me. I didn't catch on the first time through. If my parents had ever said, "Oh, it's easy," I would have been really discouraged. If it was easy and I couldn't get it, that would have meant I was really dumb. Instead, I heard the statement, "It's not so easy for you, is it? Just keep on and you'll get it. You can do it." With the help of my mom and some tutors, I did get it. I caught the notion that if I stuck with it, eventually the light would turn on for me, especially in math. That is why when I had to repeat algebra and geometry in high school, I got it the second time around. I finally got it, and it *was* easy. However, I may have never succeeded if I hadn't had someone believing in me as I struggled.

PROBLEM SOLVING WITH CHILDREN AND TEENS

Much of the time spent in parent-child or parent-teen communication is in problem solving. However, because of the lack of guidelines to follow for problem solving, often one or both parties end up frustrated. I was impressed by Dr. Paul Rosen's approach to problem solving—a technique called "TLC," which is an acronym for "Talking Listening Connecting." It is a seven-step approach and involves some known and usable problem-solving principles.[2]

Step 1: Identify the Issue

In any discussion leading to the solution of a problem, identify the issue. Clarify what you want to discuss. A vague statement, such as, "Henry, I want to talk to you," that does not state why creates either fear or an uh-oh response in the listener. Even if you're upset, take some time to calm down so that you sound calm and caring rather than angry and impatient. Here's an example:

> *Dad:* Son, I'd like to talk to you about what happened last night.
>
> *Tony:* Oh, Dad, I told you why I was late and why I

couldn't call. I said I was sorry.

Dad: I know you did. I appreciate what you said. But I want to talk about why it happened since that was the third time. It would be helpful to take some steps, so it won't occur again.

Tony: I'm not sure what to do.

Dad: Let's try to figure out some proactive steps that we agree on to take when it looks like you'll be late.

Step 2: Get Your Child's or Teen's Point of View

After you have shared what you want to talk about, let your child or teen talk. Get your child's point of view, and above all, listen. You may disagree. You may not like your child's tone or what he or she says. But don't counterattack. Don't defend. Instead, ask. Ask your child to explain his or her feelings and responses as thoroughly as possible. Encourage your child to elaborate. If you counteract what your child says at this point in the discussion, your child will stop communicating, and there won't be any resolution. Use questions and statements such as the following:

- "Tell me what happened."
- "What bothered you the most?"
- "What were some of your thoughts when that happened?"
- "How did you feel?"
- "What upset you the most?"
- "I'd like to hear more about that."
- "Help me understand this part of it."
- "It's been helpful for me to hear what you've said to me."

Notice the mom's open-ended questions in the following dialogue. Her style of questions encourages her son to elaborate and speak through his feelings.

Mom: I want to understand what made you so angry today.

Sam: You said I couldn't sleep over at Kenny's house tomorrow night.

Mom: That made you mad?

Sam: Yeah. You let Gina sleep over at her friend's house. I don't know why you said I couldn't. Why won't you let me?

Mom: I've already told you. It's not a good night for you to sleep over because we are leaving early the next day on vacation. But I don't want to talk about that right now. I want to understand why you were so mad. Why did this get to you so much?

Sam: You always say no.

Mom: Is that how you feel?

Sam: Yeah. You never let me do what I want.

Mom: Do you think I've been unfair?

Sam: Yes. All the time.

Mom: Sometimes you get angry over other things, so it's not just about me saying no.

Sam: Everything is just unfair. Gina gets to stay up later. She never gets in trouble. I'm always getting punished.

Mom: What do you feel like when you are angry?

Sam: Mad.

Mom: I know. But what's it like when you are mad?

Sam: I just can't stop it. It comes out.

Mom: What are you thinking when you get like this?

Sam: I'm not thinking about anything. I'm just mad.

Mom: How do you feel after it's over?

Sam: Better and worse.

Mom: I think I know what you mean. You don't feel as angry and that's better, but you always feel bad?

Sam: Yeah.

Mom: Do you think we should try to find another way for you to handle things when you get angry?

Sam: Yeah.

Mom: I do, too. I'm proud of you for wanting to change this. You'll feel better if you find a new way to handle your anger. I know it will help us to get along better, too.[3]

Showing empathy lets your child know that you care and understand.

Step 3: Show Empathy

This is a simple process. Showing empathy lets your child know that you care and understand. Here are some examples of statements that convey empathy:

- "I can tell you were bothered by what happened at the party."
- "The expression on your face looked painful."
- "I think most of us would feel rejected if that happened to us."
- "I wish I could take the hurt away."
- "It doesn't seem fair."

Step 4: Discuss Values

The discussion of values—your values and your child's values—is often at the heart of problem-solving discussions. You want your child or teen to develop solid values, especially spiritual values. You want to give your child guidance, and you hope your child is receptive. During discussions, you want to share your values, and then listen to your child's values. If what your child did was clearly wrong, you still don't blame. Even if your child understands the correct values, it doesn't mean he or she will always follow them. However, you can acknowledge the fact that your child knows what is best. Most important, ask, "What will you do differently next time?" and "What can you do to lock in that choice?" (Asking questions like these is a key factor to teach values and promote behavior you want.)

Remember, your child or teen *will* make mistakes. Continue to believe in your child or teen and see mistakes as lapses in judgment. Let your child know you believe that he or she has the capability of following through next time. Work with your child to make it happen, and believe that he or she can make the best choices.

Step 5: Explore Possible Solutions

If what your child or teen does isn't working, he or she needs help, which is not the same as telling him or her what to do. Instead, explore possible solutions together. Exploring is a mutual endeavor. By asking or saying one of the following examples, you can intiate exploring possible solutions with your child:

- "What do you think might work?"
- "What do you think you could do differently?"
- "What can you learn from what you tried before?"

• "I think it's great you're willing to come up with something new and try it. If it doesn't work the first time, try
it again. Then if it doesn't work again, we'll come up
with a better idea."

Discussing solutions is a joint effort. You both contribute.
The following questions also help: What makes this problem
occur? What could be done so it doesn't? What are the thoughts
you have when this happens? What other thoughts would help?

Step 6: Agree on Solutions

It is important that your child or teen feels the solution belongs
to him or her. The more ownership your child has over the
planned solution, the more he or she will follow it. Therefore,
the plan needs to be mutually agreeable. I've found it helpful to
put the plan in writing and have each person sign it. When our
daughter was 15, we put her driving agreement and a dating
agreement in writing. It made the next two years much easier,
because the guidelines were in place and we were all committed
to it.

Step 7: Follow Up and Persevere

The plans that you and your child or teen agree upon may need
refinement and reinforcement over time. Continue to express
your belief in your child's ability to change.[4]

Some children and teens express themselves better in writing
rather than by talking. This is often the case with boys.
Encourage your child to write down his or her thoughts and feelings in a letter. Don't overuse this method, but it can be a good
break from the usual routine.

Perhaps you express yourself better by talking than in writing. For a change, put a note in your child's or teen's lunch.

However, don't ask if he or she read it.

"You've got mail." E-mail is great way to get a message across. Make it creative. You could create your own code or write the message in a foreign language your child has studied. You could ask questions or send a monologue. Again, don't ask your child if he or she has read it unless you need a response. If you need a response from your child in a timely manner, make it creative like, "Need to hear from you by 4:23 P.M. and 27 seconds or the stink bomb I hid in your room will be activated. PS—It's skunk odor."

Maybe you or your child like to paint or draw. Give your child a picture depicting how you feel about something, and ask them to do the same.

Another creative way to open up the lines of communication is to give your child a fill-in-the-blank sentence to complete. Then talk about it. Do not overload your child. Only give your child one sentence each time. Here are several possibilities:

• One thing I wish I could do more of is _____
_____.

• The thing that my _____ [dad, mom, sister, etc.] does the most that really bugs me is _____
_____.

• One problem I need help solving is _____
_____.

• The thing I wish my dad would do more is _____
_____.

Feel free to create your own statements that reflect what you know your child is dealing with.[5]

Yet another way of interacting with your child creatively is to write notes such as the following:

Please pick me up, so you can walk across your room without stepping on me. Love, the stuff on the floor.

Help wanted: clean bathroom, close shampoo bottle, cap toothpaste tube, hang up wet towels. Reward: a very pleased mother.

Help! Please take me out before I overflow. Love, the trash.[6]

THE RULES

Here is an example of a written contract one mother developed for her 9- and 11-year-old sons. I know the family very well. This approach worked!

Dear Hayden and C. J.,

As we start this summer, I want you to know how proud I am of each of you. You are both growing up to be respectful, helpful and courteous young men. But I also want you to know that although your boundaries are getting bigger and you have more privileges this summer, there will still be rules. Please read the following rules and initial after each rule. If you agree, then please sign at the bottom of the letter. Your signature acknowledges that you are aware of these rules and of their consequences.

1. Do not leave the house until you have looked me in the eye and heard me say yes. Please tell me specifically where you are going, and if you go somewhere else, please make sure I know how to find you imme-

diately. You can either call me or come back home and look me in the eye to tell me. There will be no yelling from the street in hopes that I might hear you. I need to know.

If you do leave and I cannot find you: first offense—write or say 12 "I will not leave without telling Mom" sentences; second offense—write or say 24 "I will not leave without telling Mom" sentences; third offense—stay inside one hour with no TV and no games, and without asking me, "What can I do?"; fourth offense and so on—Dad will choose the consequence.

Initials _____   _____

2. If my bedroom door is shut, it means that I need a few minutes of privacy. Please do not enter unless your life is in jeopardy, which means only if you are bleeding, swelling or possibly dying. Otherwise, I will come out within 20 minutes. I know you can wait 20 minutes. You may knock and ask me a question, but if I am showering, *wait* until I open the door for you.

If you ignore my right to privacy: first offense—write or say 12 "I will give Mom a break" sentences; second offense—write or say 24 "I will give Mom a break" sentences; third offense—stay inside one hour with no TV and no games, and without asking me, "What can I do?"; fourth offense and so on—stay inside an additional hour for each additional offense.

Initials _____   _____

3. Talking back is a no-no. That means when I say I need to do an errand, you will get in the car without question and go. Errands usually will last one hour

or less, and then you'll be able to come home and continue playing with your friends. When I ask you to empty the trash, empty the dishwasher, pick up your bedroom, and so on, you will not tell me that your brother should do it, nor will you ignore me and act like you didn't hear me. Your chores usually take 5 to 10 minutes at the most. This brief time-out from playing or lying around watching TV will not end your life. In fact, I believe it might make you a better person. There are other instances when you may find yourself wanting to talk back; instead, hold your tongue!

If you talk back: first offense—write or say 12 "I will not talk back to my parents" sentences; second offense—write or say 24 "I will not talk back to my parents" sentences; third offense—stay inside one hour with no TV and no games, and without asking me, "What can I do?"; fourth offense and so on—stay inside an additional hour for each additional offense.

Initials _____   _____

4. You are both very capable of making wise decisions. You are both very smart young men. And I believe that on your own you know things such as not to play with fire, not to destroy someone else's property and to wear a helmet when riding a skateboard, bike, scooter and so on. However, there are times when your good judgment may get the best of you.

In those cases: first offense—write or say 12 "I will think twice" sentences; second offense—write or say 24 "I will think twice" sentences; third offense—stay inside one hour with no TV and no games, and without asking me, "What can I do?"; fourth offense and so on—stay inside an additional hour for each additional offense.

Initials _____   _____

There may be more rules added to this list as the summer goes on. But this is a start. Truly, I believe that you're both wise enough to get them right away. If you do get busted for any of the above and you give me flack regarding the consequence, your writing consequence will increase by 10 sentences until you calm down and start writing, and your time inside will increase by 15 minutes until you settle down and do your time.

We can all have a great summer! Summer is meant to be fun! It is a time for doing fun things with friends and playing hard. This is what I want your summer to be like. You know, the kind of summer that when you're 20, you'll look back and say, "We always had fun summers!"

Please sign below to acknowledge your understanding of the above.

I love you both,
Mom

THE APPROPRIATE QUESTIONS

Most of us parents ask too many questions for which there are no good replies. We hint through our questions or assume our children will catch on and respond in the way we want. Communication doesn't work that way.

You can ask any question and make it say what you want. You could call this question a statement, request, command or whatever else. It can be phrased politely, briefly and firmly.

If you say, "Please don't touch that again," a child hears, "This is what I want. There's no other option—no negotiating. And if there isn't compliance, there will be consequences." These may need to be added to your phrase the next time, but it's better to point toward what you would like the child to do.

There is another variation of negative questions, which have a very self-defeating aspect. What do the following questions say?

- Don't you want to go shopping with me?
- Don't you want to sit on the couch with me?
- Can't you remember what I asked you to do for one minute?
- Can't you follow instructions?

Most of us parents ask too many questions for which there are no good replies.

Do you see the two problems with these questions? First, the questions don't say what the parent really wants. Second, each question is a negative suggestion and leaves a sense of doubt. You really see this when you turn each question into a statement. Just switch the first two words and see the result.[7]

Table 5.1 lists six examples of negative questions. Notice how the child mentally reacts to the question, what the parent actually meant to say and what the child ultimately does in response to the negative question.

Table 5.1

Negative Questions

Parent Says	Child Thinks	Parent Meant	Child Does
"What did I just say?"	*You said, "Don't touch that again."*	"Don't touch that again!"	Touches it anyway.
"How many times have I told you to knock it off?"	*Five, 10, 20 times—who knows?*	"Keep your feet off your brother's chair!"	Kicks his brother's chair again.
"How about leaving your sister alone for a change?"	*Well, how about it?*	"Don't interrupt your sister's reading. Leave her alone!"	Bugs his sister again.
"Don't you want to finish your squash?"	*No. I hate squash.*	"Eat the rest of your food."	Continues to stare at her plate.
"Didn't you ask me to take you to this movie?"	*Yep, I did.*	"Be quiet and stop bothering all the people around us."	Continues to talk and bug her neighbor.
"Can you say, 'Thank you'?"	*Yes, I can.*	"Say, 'Thank you,' to the nice lady."	Says nothing.

Source: Denis Donovan, M.D., M.Ed., and Deborah McIntyre, M.A., R.N., *What Did I Just Say!?!* (New York: Henry Holt and Co., 1999), pp. 13-14.

A THOUGHT FOR TODAY

If you're a parent, perhaps you'll identify with this brief essay:

It's been one of those days. Hectic, hurried, and hassled. You couldn't stop for a minute; you would have been run over. They were all right behind you waiting for you to stumble—deadlines, dishes, the dentist, duties waiting to devour you if you dallied just for a moment. It seemed that everyone and everything from the kids to the endless phone interruptions wanted a piece of you. When one task was completed (or just started) the next one raised its head demanding to be noticed. A spilled plate (full of food), the dog's dish overturned, the stopped-up toilet, and the forgotten child crying and waiting at school to be picked up and taken to practice all seemed to make your day . . . worse. In the midst of it all you wondered, *Will it ever end? Where will I find more time? What else can go wrong? How can I hurry more?*

But wait! Hold it. Hurrying isn't the answer. It won't help. It won't work. It will stress you out more and build a sense of panic. What you want to do is slow down. Yes, that's what I said: slow down. In fact, when your day is coming apart and you're running around in circles, stop. Hold everything. Sit down in a comfortable chair, take a deep breath and . . . read the following prayer:

Steady my hurried pace with a vision of the eternal reach of time.

Give me, amid the confusion of the day, the calmness of the everlasting hills.

Break the tensions of my nerves and muscles with the soothing music of the singing streams that live in my memory.

Teach me the art of taking minute vacations—of slowing down to look at a flower, to chat with a friend, to pat a dog, to smile at a child, to read a few lines from a good book.

Slow me down, Lord, and inspire me to send my roots deep into the soil of life's enduring values, that I may grow toward my greater destiny.

Remind me each day that the race is not always to the swift; that there is more to life than increasing its speed.

Let me look upward to the towering oak and know that it grew great and strong because it grew slowly and well.[8]

CHAPTER 6

Commonsense Guidelines for Effective Communication

I'm tired of trying to get through to my kids. They're 9, 11 and 14. I make requests and all I get are arguments or hassles. They badger me with their requests, and I do the same. Is there a better way to get across what I want?

Yes, there are ways that work. But two things have to occur: (1) change what you've been doing if it isn't working, and (2) be stubbornly consistent.

MAKE YOUR REQUESTS CRYSTAL CLEAR

One reason parents cave in to their children's requests is because they become weary. What they do to get through to their children or to motivate them doesn't work. To get rid of the hassle, they throw in the towel. When you make a request to your child, make your communication crystal clear. Don't be vague.

Often parents begin with *unclear* requests or directions. What may be obvious to them isn't clear to their children.

Children can't read their parents' minds. Parents often communicate vague or tentative requests, or they say too much or express themselves in a way their children don't understand. What about it? Have *you* ever been on the receiving end of unclear requests or directions? If so, did you feel like complying? Probably not. And neither will your child. "Don't eat too much." "Don't stay out too late." "Don't play too rough." What do these requests mean? What is "too much," "too late," "too rough"? You can't measure these phrases. When you confront your child for violating these requests, you're probably going to get an argument. Your child's idea of "too much" is different from your idea. Instead, you need to spell it out.

Be Specific

When you make a request, make it clear and simple, and focus on your child's behavior, not his or her character. This is healthy communication. For any child to follow through with your requests, you must be specific. General, vague comments like, "Do a good job on the lawn," or "Get home at a reasonable time,"—a great one for a teen—are not enforceable. Instead, use specific language in your comments such as, "Dinner is at 5:30 P.M. Please be here by 5:15 P.M. to help," or "When you clean your room, put all dirty clothes in the hamper, all clean clothes on hangers and dust every piece of furniture." These requests give your child a specific message of what you expect from him or her. Your message needs to state exact times like: "now," "right away" or "by ___ o'clock."

Avoid Repetition

For some reason, we as parents feel the need to repeat what we've said. Doing this teaches a child or teen *not* to listen. Did you ever think of that? You may help to create the very thing you don't want to happen. If you feel you have to repeat, you probably believe you are not being listened to or you are being ignored. That's not a pleasant experience. When we repeat, we usually use the same language but intensify the presentation a bit. However, if what you said the first time didn't register, why would you believe saying it again will work?

If something needs repeating, it needs to be *repackaged*— that's the key. Get your child's attention by going to where your child is (i.e., not talking from room to room), put your hand gently on your child's shoulder and speak softly and slowly. Then I think you will be heard. Remember, if it's your son you're talking to, he probably has difficulty doing more than one thing at a time. It's vital that he stop what he's doing in order for your message to connect with him. When I give a command softly to my golden retrievers, I usually get an immediate response. They know the tone I'm using means they need to respond. The key is to lower your voice. Make it soft. A firm and soft voice is an attention getter.

A firm and soft voice is an attention getter.

Eliminate Reminders

Reminding is similar to repeating. Every time we remind someone, we feed our own irritation. It takes energy to remind, and the older our children, the more irritation we experience. "Why can't he remember anything I say? He's 15!" If we constantly remind, our children get *us* to take responsibility for their lack of responsibility. For example, when our children forget to take their lunch, coat, food money or book to school and we rush in to bail them out, we feel more of an urgency to remind them the next time, which gives them less of a reason to remember. Additionally, we reinforce their forgetfulness by bailing them out.

By the way, most children have a very effective weapon they use when we repeat or remind: They ignore us. And no one likes to be ignored.

Be Consistent

Sometimes the reason our children don't respond is because they know we don't mean what we say. They know "right now" means "anytime." They know "not until you've done your chores" means "now." And the worst one is when they know that our "no" means "yes" or "maybe"! When our children believe that complying with our requests is optional, our limits are not clear or strong enough. The words we use need to reflect their meaning or we shouldn't use them. If our children or teens can't depend on our meaning what we say about simple requests, should they believe what we say about values?

Here's a common experience. Have you ever told your child to turn the radio, TV or computer down or off and heard, "Yeah, I will" or "In a minute." Those responses usually mean just the opposite, and when you remind, you usually get the same response. It doesn't have to be that way. There are many children and teens who learn to respond to the first request. They learned early on that noncompliance meant their parents would take action. They learned they could depend on their parents to follow through with what they said. What have those parents done? They made eye contact with their children;

they made their requests clear and concise; they asked their children to report what was said; and they gave directions according to their children's ability to remember. This is child-speak. It's also teenspeak. It works.

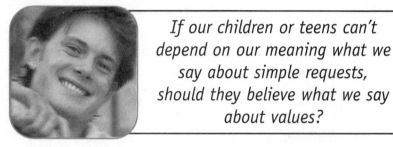

If our children or teens can't depend on our meaning what we say about simple requests, should they believe what we say about values?

Remember, every child or teen is wired or created in a unique way. Some children have the ability to remember more for a long period of time. Others forget half of what was said on the way to their room. More forgetful children need smaller pieces of information. They can handle small doses. For more details on children's different personality types, see David Stoop's *Understanding Your Child's Personality* (Tyndale House Publishers, 1998).[1]

Some parents (if their children are old enough to read) give their children instructions in writing, because many children are visual learners. This works especially with boys, as most boys are visual learners.

Don't Give Multiple Reasons

Some parents place great value on giving reasons: "I want my son to understand the rationale for what I'm asking him to do" or "I always thought if my daughter knew the reasons for what I asked, she would be more cooperative." Our reasons make sense to us but may not to our children. All the reasons in the world may not help if our children don't want to cooperate. Yes, it's true, we do give reasons initially so that our children learn. But once is enough. We don't need to go over them again and again. It's like an appeal, but it doesn't help. Responding to our children's why questions is not necessary if we clearly explained it once. Children use these questions as a stall tactic and as an expression of resistance. We need to be careful that we do not overexplain to our children. Not every question needs or deserves an explanation. Some parents list their reasons in writing if their children are old enough to read. This helps some, and it is a form of communication. Other parents tell their children to take a time-out and take that time to think back to what the reasons were the first time they explained them. This helps, too, and is another form of communication. One parent said, "Oh, it was so exasperating. My son would say, 'Why?' and I would explain, and he would say it again. The message I received was that my answer wasn't good enough for him." Continual why's or arguments leave this message: Your reasons aren't good enough for me.

Skip the Bargaining and the Quarrels

Do you enjoy bargaining as a means of communication? There are some cultures where you *never* pay the initial price quoted to you—it would be an insult to do so. Some children must think they're part of that culture! They constantly try to bargain with you. If a child persists, pleads, whines and digs in his or her heels and you begin to waiver, concede and finally bend, the child learns a lesson. The child learns he or she can win, and the child begins to establish a pattern the child can use the rest of his or her life. The child learns a dysfunctional form of communication. The child learns to argue, and sometimes these encounters turn ugly and become quarrels. Scripture has something to say about this:

To quarrel with a neighbor is foolish; a man with good sense holds his tongue (Prov. 11:12, *TLB*).

Starting a quarrel is like a leak in a dam, so stop it before a fight breaks out (Prov. 17:14, *NCV*).

Foolish people are always fighting, but avoiding quarrels will bring you honor (Prov. 20:3, *NCV*).

If it is possible, as far as it depends on you, live at peace with everyone (Rom. 12:18, *NIV*).

Get rid of all bitterness, rage and anger, brawling and slander, along with every form of malice (Eph. 4:31, *NIV*).

How do you stay out of bargaining and quarrels? How do you stay out of getting worn down? Years ago I learned an approach called the broken-record technique. Depending on your age, you may remember what a broken record is. Today we have CDs, and we still have audiocassettes, but we used to have eight tracks, and records—round plastic disks that you placed a needle on to create the sound. (Have your kids ever see one of these?) When a record turned on the turntable and the needle got stuck, it kept playing the same phrase over and over again until you stopped it—you couldn't fast-forward. Well, the same principle has been applied in communication—and it's highly effective. By repeating the same response over and over, the other person will eventually give up. When someone is trying to persuade you to change your mind, to purchase something or to do something, all you have to do is employ the broken-record technique and you'll win. Most people can't last against this defense.

If someone pressures you to buy something and tries to find out why you won't buy it (you don't have to give in and you shouldn't give in), all you have to say is, "No, thank you. I'm just not interested," again and again and again. If a friend pressures you to attend something and you don't want to go, all you have to say is, "Thank you for asking, but I'm unable to attend." You don't have to give a reason.

Here is an example of bargaining. You asked your son to clean his room before he goes swimming over at his friend's place, and he agreed. But it hasn't happened yet. Jimmy runs by, and the following conversation takes place:

> *Jimmy:* See ya, Mom. I'm going over to Ken's to swim.
> *Mom:* Wait up, Jimmy. You said earlier that you would clean your room before you went to Ken's.
> *Jimmy:* But Mom, I need to leave now. It would take too long to clean it.
> *Mom:* That may be the case, Jimmy, and feel free to go when your room is clean.
> *Jimmy:* Mom, Ken called and wants to show me stuff before the others get there.
> *Mom:* I'm sure he did, and feel free to go as soon as your room is clean.
> *Jimmy:* Why can't I do it later? Other kids get to play first and then they do their work. It's not fair.
> *Mom:* That may be true, Jimmy, and feel free to go after your room is clean.[2]

Jimmy cleaned his room. Mom didn't go ballistic, raise her voice or get angry. Mom spoke a quiet, controlled, persistent, determined statement that deflected every onslaught Jimmy sent her way. Did you notice how I described Mom's statement?

Quiet, controlled, persistent and determined. You can do the same thing. Can you think of phrases you could use? Write out some of the statements that your child uses on you and practice your response in advance. Use phrases like "Feel free to . . . " or "You're welcome to go when . . . "

Remember, you're not threatening. You're not badgering. You're not bargaining. You're simply calling your child back to your request and his or her agreement. You're helping your child learn how to follow through and become trustworthy. You also can use statements like "We've talked about this enough. Please don't bring it up again. If you do . . . " or "It's time for action. You can do what I asked or . . . What would you like to do?" Please note: Use short, concise responses.

IMPLEMENT TWO-WAY COMMUNICATION

Sometimes parent-child interaction becomes a one-way process. However, communication is a two-way process. Parents use one approach quite frequently, which actually blocks the communication process. It is called *lecturing* and is employed when parents don't think their children are listening or when their children disobey. Lecturing, in this instance, is not considered a positive action. Instead, it refers to when parents try to correct children by teaching, giving all the facts, pointing out wrongdoing and questioning whether their brain is in gear. All the time the parents hope that this approach solves the problem once and for all. I call this approach, "tell them, teach them and they'll shape up." It's not the best way to handle parent-child communication, and it violates Scripture:

> The smart person says very little, and one with understanding stays calm. Even fools seem to be wise if they

keep quiet; if they don't speak, they appear to understand (Prov. 17:27-28, *NCV*).

Those who are careful about what they say keep themselves out of trouble (Prov. 21:23, *NCV*).

For a child or teen to learn something, he or she has to listen, want to learn, be open to change and be excited about discovering something new. I don't think this is the attitude of most children when their parents lecture them. They usually wait out the tirade by sighing, rolling their eyes, looking at their watch or tapping their feet.

Talk Less

There is a communication principle that effective parents have learned to follow. If they want to be heard by their children more, *they talk less*. That's right. Less accomplishes more. The greater the amount of words that come out of the mouth, the more children's ears and mouths close. A malady seems to hit children when parents lecture. It's called PLG, which stands for parent lecture gaze. As one child said, "I go into my *Night of the Living Dead* stare." Children's eyes begin to gloss over when parents start in, and even more so if they know it's lecture number 17. (Teens are really good at deciphering lecture topics.) Oh, children may grunt every four or five minutes just to let their parents know they're awake. Kids see a lecture as a long *one-sided* interchange with comments like, "Now, see here" or "You need to listen, young man" or "and furthermore."

Parents tell me time and time again that they have trouble getting their children to listen. Can children really listen? Yes, they can. Try the following:

1. Be sure you get your child's attention. Your child needs to listen to you with his or her eyes, since non-verbal communication accounts for 5 percent of a message.

2. Let your child know you're only going to be talking for 93 seconds (about 1½ minutes). Look at your watch and keep time.

3. Don't give a big answer to your child's little question.

4. Use the "one-word rule." That's right, say one word and no more. If your child or teen comes and drops his or her coat on the floor or chair, instead of saying, "How many times have I told you . . . ?" just say, "Coat!" If your daughter forgets to turn out the lights, just say, "Lights." Save your words; you'll have better responses. However, to make this work, you need to practice, practice and practice some more. Identify what you want to say and practice out loud. You can use gestures and the raised eyebrow to make your point.[3]

When we firmly say, "I want to talk to you," often our children have a tense here-we-go-again look on their face. A lecture is an example of the law of diminishing returns. *The more said, the less heard.* Remember, the older a child, the more his or her definition of a lecture changes. To a teen, it's probably any input over 10 words![4]

Reinforce Good Behavior

There's something else to consider: If you lecture and rehash your child's problem, you tend to reinforce and heighten the probability that it will happen again. This does not solve the problem. Instead, you could ask your child, "What was our original agreement?" and no matter what tactic your child takes to avoid answering, you can keep repeating the question in a calm voice. If you get the classic response, "I don't know," just say, "When you remember, then we can continue our conversation and the day's activities. Let me know when you remember." If your child is an introvert, be sure to say, "Take some time to think about it." Remember, an introvert child has to think in the privacy of his or her own mind before he or she can speak. You won't get any response if you put pressure on an introvert child. It's not a defect; it's just the way the child was created.

Instead of rehashing your child's problem and lecturing, talk about what you would like your child to do differently the next time. You are more likely to see a change when you focus on the positive. If you point toward the desired behavior, which will be the last message your child hears, your child will be more likely to follow through with the desired behavior. Make your words count. Your child will hear them.

Furthermore, when your child follows your instructions or directions, let your child know how much you appreciate his or her behavior: "I really like it when you choose to follow directions the first time." When you affirm your child's positive behavior, you send a message that you believe your child is capable of doing what you ask. You didn't plead, bargain, lecture or fall into any other poor communication trap.[5]

Interpret Eye Movement

When you try to get something across to your child, have you ever noticed what your child's eyes are doing? Some kids look up; some look to the side; some look down. When you see your child's eyes elsewhere, his or her mind is elsewhere as well. However, your child's eye movement will tell you what's going on in his or her mind! Eyes are a doorway to your child's thoughts. Your child's eye movements are not random; they're purposeful.

For example, if your child rolls his or her eyes *up* and to the *right*, your child is probably in the process of constructing a visual image. But if the eyes are going *up* and to the *left*, your child probably recalls a previous image. Radical? No. Haven't you rolled your own eyes? Probably, but you've just not thought about it that much.

> *When you affirm your child's positive behavior, you send a message that you believe your child is capable of doing what you ask.*

What if your child keeps his or her eyes *level* and to the *right*? Your child is probably in the process of constructing sounds. Your child talks silently while you talk out loud. If the eyes are *level* and to the *left*, your child probably remembers previously heard sounds.

If your child looks *down* and to the *right*, your child is probably experiencing certain feelings. If the eyes are *down* and to the *left*, your child is probably talking to himself or herself. (Keep in mind that many left-handed individuals are reversed right to left).[6]

How will this help you? Many of you who notice your child's straying eyes ask, "Are you listening to me?" or "What are you thinking about now?" Instead, you might ask a question like the following:

• "What are you seeing in your mind right now?" or "What picture is coming to your mind?" if your child looks *up* and to the *right*.

- "What picture from your photo album popped into your mind right now?" if your child looks *up* and to the *left*. They might look at you and say, "Wow! How did you know?" Now you're connecting.
- "Are you beginning to hear how this sounds?" if your child's eyes are *level* and to the *right*.
- "What are you remembering hearing right now?" if your child's eyes are *level* and to the *left*.
- "Are you feeling something at this time?" or "Are you sensing something right now?" if your child looks *down* and to the *right*.
- "What are you saying to yourself right now?" if your child looks *down* and to the *left*.

Before you think these ideas are too bizarre, try experimenting with them. As you experiment, you'll become aware of your own eye movements and what may be going on inside of you.

Stop Yelling

Many parents yell. They raise their voices to get their point across. Some parents say, "Hey, it's just part of our cultural heritage. It's the way we were raised." Have you ever been yelled at? Has someone raised his or her voice at you? If so, how did you feel? Did you remember what you were supposed to? Did you want to follow through with what the person wanted from you, or did you feel more like digging in your heels? Did you want a better or closer relationship with this person? No is probably the answer to most of these questions. This is probably how a child feels when a parent *raises his or her voice* or *yells*. Yelling also shows that the parent has lost control. If your face gets red and your veins pop out and you're on the verge of hysteria, your child is probably enjoying the show. Remember, in some states, yelling is considered emotional abuse.

Being loud and intense can be different from yelling if the emotion behind it is not anger. Usually the emotion behind yelling is anger. Few people want to draw close to an angry person. If a parent is nearly over the edge with frustration and anger, he or she is more likely to exert physical abuse.

Yelling at your child doesn't give you greater control; instead, it numbs your child's heart toward you. Your child will be less willing to listen and cooperate. As you increase the volume, your child's ability to hear diminishes.

If your child does respond, it's usually out of fear and intimidation, and very little lasting learning occurs. I don't know many parents who are proud to say, "My child is afraid of me."

Lower your voice. Use your tone creatively. These work wonders.[7]

CHAPTER 7

Adolescence Happens

It happens. It may be gradual, or it may occur overnight. The child that you could talk to is now a stranger, who responds to you as if you're from outer space. Welcome to the world of adolescence. Communication changes from talking and joking to a sullen or ashen silence.

In the book *Eight Seasons of Parenthood,* the season of adolescence is coined, "The Volcano Years." It's unpredictable. It's never dull. As a parent you are personally challenged on all levels—physically, spiritually, intellectually and emotionally—by the change. Some parents hate it and would like to have an adolescent bypass operation. They want to "live on solid ground again." Other parents love this time:

> They loved living on the rim of active volcanoes, loved never knowing if, at the ring of the phone or emergence of a zit, their formerly sane children would have eruptions of insanity, spew forth lava, and go up in flames. They loved being the rescue crew, there to clean up the molten rocks and ash from their children's lives. It made them, in some ways, continue to feel needed.[1]

When adolescence hits, there are changes that no one ever

talks about. For example, when your child becomes a teen, his or her intelligence increases. Just ask. Your teen seems to know almost everything there is to know. And your teen's friends' intelligence also increases, which seems to be whom your teen listens to. Your teen's communication with you as a parent shrinks to as few words as possible.

Your teen's room becomes his or her cave. Your teen wants privacy, sleep and escape from adults.

Gadgets are your teen's life—CDs, cell phones and anything associated with his or her computer.

You can expect mood swings, an overreliance on his or her peers and a dress code that baffles you. You will be confronted with driving, dating, sex, tattoos and body piercing, to name a few. These are adolescent changes. But from *your teen's* perspective, you have changed.

One author describes the process that takes place during adolescence:

> Although there is no scientific evidence to back the theory, it seems as if the energy that is required for the child to develop physically during adolescence seems to be drained directly from the parents' brains. The end result is that we lose IQ points and become less intelligent than when the child was nine or ten years old. Because of this loss in intelligence, our logic and reasoning become faulty. We approach life and the world from a very limited capacity and our ability to adequately provide information and direction is significantly reduced. In other words, we get dumber and do not know what we're talking about.[2]

At least that's the way the teen sees us!

For some reason the adolescent doesn't want to be seen with

his or her parents. They're an embarrassment to the teen. The teen thinks the way his or her parents talk, act and dress have changed for the worse. To the teen, his or her parents are either senile or suffer from amnesia. They've forgotten what it's like to be a teen. They just don't understand. They forget and tend to tell their teen the same thing again and again.

Is it any wonder that you have to work harder at communication? Fortunately, these changes occur in varying degrees with each teen. There are some teens who hit these changes like an intermittent speed bump in the road and move into early adulthood rapidly.[3] Other teens amble into early adulthood like a snail.

Remember that during adolescence communication usually decreases and the teen confides less in his or her parents. This is normal; don't take it personally.

COMMUNICATION HURDLES

Remember that during adolescence communication usually decreases and the teen confides less in his or her parents. This is normal; don't take it personally. (Yes, there *are* exceptions, and you will hope your family is the exception.)

With a teen, casual listening is much better than logical arguments or retaliations. This is a time to listen for feelings and draw them out.

Teens hate it when they talk with their parents and don't have 110 percent of their attention. They need to see your face looking at them.

Additionally, you have a greater chance of staying connected if most of what you say is positive rather than negative.

Focusing on successes, accomplishments and interests works better than focusing on mistakes and failures. One father asked his teen, "John, I don't like to talk about lapses or mistakes. Sometimes I need to. Tell me the best way to put it, and I'll follow that and keep it short. I'd much rather talk about what's working."

Talk to teens especially about their interests. For years I worked as a youth pastor. Often I had a car full of teens. Much of the time I just kept quiet and listened. The kids were amazed at how much I knew about their lives. Why should they be surprised? They told me.

Start thinking about how your teen expects you to talk to him or her. And don't be predictable. It is better to say less than too much.

Finally, when you talk to your teen, let him or her know "because of your advanced age and sensitivity to distortion, you need to talk with your teen without the competition of the TV, stereo or the Internet. You will become sane as the conversation progresses." It has worked for many.

FLUCTUATING FEELINGS

Adolescents live in a world of fluctuating feelings. You may not agree with what your teen feels. However, try to understand what your teen feels. Don't try to fix your teen or explain away his or her feelings. Just be there.

Are you a reactor? If yes, your teen will know it and exploit it. They love to get reactions. Therefore, slow down, do the unexpected and delay your response. If your teen is angry, say, "I want to hear what you have to say. Speak slower, so I can catch it." Often your teen's anger will diminish.

Some teens constantly push for immediate answers. One

parent used this approach: "If I have to give you an answer now, it will be no. I don't necessarily want it to be no. If I have time to think about it, there is as much possibility for a yes as there is a no. Which do you prefer?" By delaying your response like this, your answer will not be based on your feelings or your teen's.

You may not agree with what your teen feels. However, try to understand what your teen feels.

LAND MINES

There are three "land mines" that destroy a parent-teen relationship. When a land mine blows, no one wins. In each land mine, it takes two to play. If one person doesn't engage, land mines don't occur. The three land mines are arguments, confrontations and power struggles. When you engage in these, you lose.[4]

If these land mines occur on a regular basis, you need to identify the following:

1. Where do the arguments, confrontations or power struggles occur? What room or location?
2. When do they occur? Some parents have said just before or after dinner, or just before they leave for work. To break this pattern, establish a rule in the house that says crucial issues cannot be discussed during the half hour prior to or after dinner, or just before work. They can be brought up at [list a more appropriate time].

If land mines occur in the kitchen, the teen's room or your bedroom, establish these areas as off-limits. Instead, establish a safe room—a neutral area such as the bathroom—for crucial discussions. One person can sit on the tub and the other person can sit on the toilet. Or try the car where both people sit in the backseat, or the laundry room where one person sits on the washer and the other person sits on the dryer.

One family became very creative. Whoever was talking sat on the washer and the other person sat on the dryer. They kept switching back and forth. Actually, it may sound silly, but it worked off nervous energy and kept the discussions short.

I've said this before, but it bears repeating especially with adolescents: The less said, the better. One way to stay out of situations that lead to land mines is to establish clear rules. Remember, the rules need to apply to everyone. The following are examples of rules:

The car won't run without gas. If it's brought back on empty, it's not available for the next three days.

I serve dinner between 5:30 P.M. and 6:30 P.M. The kitchen closes at 6:30 P.M. Anyone who eats after 6:30 P.M. fixes their own dinner.

Clothes that I find in the hamper will be washed. If you do not use the hamper, either wear your clothes dirty or do your own wash.

Chores need to be completed on time. If not, someone else will do them, and you'll need to pay the person for his or her time.

We are available to discuss money Monday through Thursday between 7:00 P.M. and 7:30 P.M. Please plan for these times since your financial consultants are not available at any other time.[5]

SILENCE

What if your teen won't talk to you? Expect this to happen at times. This is part of the unpredictability of adolescence. It happens when you least expect it. It's unusual for a teen to share everything with a parent. If your teen shuts down, it may not be anything you've said or done—it's just adolescence. Here are some reasons for why your teen may not share with you from the authors of *Parenting Teens with Love and Logic*:

They may not feel safe sharing certain things with you. Our dream is they could talk about anything and everything. But that's a dream—they probably won't share embarrassing thoughts, problems or situations with you because they think you wouldn't be able to handle what you hear. If you're an advice-giver this will be more likely. They don't want advice or judgment of themselves or their friends. There's a phrase all of us as parents need to practice, memorize and use. It's "I'm glad you shared that with me. What kind of response are you looking for from me?" Adolescents don't talk because they're trying to become independent. Their thought is, "If I share everything, I give them more control and I'm not independent."

There's another reason for holding back. Many aren't sure how to say what's going on in their life. This is especially true when it comes to describing feelings they're experiencing.

Remember the difference between a child and adolescent? The key word is "change"—the physical, emotional and chemical changes going on in a teen's body are overwhelming and they can't always handle them.

Sometimes an adolescent thinks, "I'm the only one struggling with this thought or problem. I can't tell anyone. They'll think I'm weird or crazy." And their next thought is, "Something is wrong with me."

There are three guidelines to follow that will help:

1. Don't interrogate and hit your adolescent with a bombardment of questions. Will your questions encourage or discourage him or her to talk?
2. Create an atmosphere of safety to talk. Anger and criticism will put a damper on the conversation quicker than anything.
3. Don't try to force him or her to talk. It creates a power struggle and pushes them away. They'll talk when they're ready and feel safe.[6]

GUNPOWDER TOPICS

"Gunpowder"—the very word brings to mind noise, destruction and intensity. When your child hits adolescence, you and your teen will talk about certain issues. Some people label these issues as gunpowder topics, because they have the potential to be explosive. Let's name a few: body piercing, clothes, contraception, curfew, dating, drinking, drugs, Internet, sex and tattoos. You know, just some of the typical, everyday adolescent issues. You can't avoid these issues. You can't *not* talk about them. But in many homes when these issues arise, it's not a discussion but an intense reaction from the parents.

Much of the reason for this intense reaction is that parents aren't sure how to handle some of these discussions. Parents don't think much about the issues in advance, so when they're confronted by these issues they're taken off guard.

Chores

Let's begin with a couple of less volatile issues and see how you would discuss them. Let's start with one of the teen's least favorite topics—chores. Most teens don't care to do chores and think they have to do more than their friends and siblings. If your teen comes to you and complains about his or her chores, consider what you would say.

Remember, you want to respond in such a way that you keep the communication flowing. Some parents fall into the trap of making comments such as the following:

- "Don't be so lazy."
- "You do your chores or you're grounded."
- "I wish you were like Jimmy next door."
- "You're getting off easy. I did five times this much as a kid."

Responses that keep the discussion going:

- "Tell me what you think you could be doing for chores."
- "How much time a week do you think would be fair for doing chores?"
- "Since we all have to do chores, are there certain ones you prefer?"
- "Let's list everyone's chores for the week and then evaluate."

- "Tell me what it is you're supposed to do each day."
- "There are certain chores that must be done and some we need to hire someone to do. That person could be you."
- "You don't like us reminding you to do your chores. Think about it and then tell me your plan for reminding yourself."

Clothes

Now, let's tackle your teen's clothes. Perhaps you'd prefer to toss them out. Teens usually want to dress in the style of their friends. It's a matter of belonging to a group, and clothes become the "uniform." On a scale of 0 to 10 in importance, clothes are probably a 12! When you think of the style of clothes your teen likes, what words come to mind? How would your teen describe his or her clothes?

Here are some typical statements that parents make about clothes, which aren't effective when dealing with teens:

- "As long as you're in this house, you'll wear what we decide. We pay for the clothes."
- "Don't buy your clothes just for the label."
- "You're not going to hang around kids who dress like that."
- "You look terrible in those clothes. Don't you care what others think of you?"

One of the best suggestions I've found on this subject comes from Dr. Richard Heyman's *How to Say It to Teens*. When purchasing your teen's clothing, Dr. Heyman suggests separating your teen's clothing into two types: needs and wants. You have an idea of what the *needs* are. Some of your teen's *wants* may include some *needs* items, but they might be a "certain" kind with a higher price tag. Some parents suggest to their teens that the teens pay the difference for their more expensive choices.

Dr. Heyman suggests the following guidelines and what to say:

- "You can wear anything as long as it's not illegal, immoral, dangerous or dirty."
- "Let's talk about what you need and what you want."
- "We'll pay for your needs and you can choose the style."
- "Let's talk about your clothing wants and how you would pay for them."
- "When you're going out with us, we expect you to dress appropriately."
- "When you dress, be sure others get the impression that you intend for them to get."[7]

Contraception

How would you respond if your teen came to you and asked, "What's the best type of contraceptive?" How would you respond if you found contraceptives in your son's jeans or your daughter's purse?

Have you shared with your teen what you believe is appropriate sexual behavior and why? Can you articulate adequate reasons? Do you have a clear understanding of the teachings of Scripture?

One father asked his son to think about the following questions, and then they spent time discussing their responses:

- If you could ask one question about sex, what would it be? (Yes, there *are* some teens who would engage in such a discussion.)

- What are the different means of contraception and how reliable are they in preventing disease?
- What are the pressures to have sex that teens struggle with today?
- What questions would you like to have answered about sex and who could help you with these questions?
- If a person wants to wait until he or she marries to experience sex, what can the person do to keep his or her standards?

Following the discussion, this is what the parent shared:

There's a lot of sexual pressure today. We see it all around us. Even when couples marry, there's still pressure. You know that our values are based upon Scripture, and we trust these are your values. For us contraception means abstinence—no sex until marriage. Many engage in unprotected sex, and not only does this lead to pregnancy, but it also leads to various sexual diseases. Even when the pill or a condom is used, it's not 100 percent effective against certain diseases or pregnancy. I realize that it may not be easy to talk to us about this, so I want to give you the names of a couple of people you can talk with who are knowledgeable in this area. If any of your friends are struggling with this, they can talk with these people as well.

Curfew

Do you have a curfew for your teen? If so, why? Your teen will ask. Perhaps you want your teen to get enough sleep, so he or she is rested for the next day. Perhaps your teen broke your trust and he or she needs to rebuild it. Or maybe your teen is being disciplined.

When you respond, don't say, "Hey, we set the rules here in this house!" or "It's for your own good, so don't tell me about your friend's curfew." These statements won't help your relationship.

Your teen will challenge the curfew you enforce, and he or she will give a multitude of reasons. Hear your teen out. Some parents ask their teens to submit a curfew request in writing. This includes *suggestions* for curfew times, reasons for these times, solutions to parental concerns and a suggested time period for a trial of these guidelines with an evaluation at the conclusion. The parents do the same. Then the family sits down and negotiates.

Here is a suggested statement:

> We set a curfew so you can get the sleep you need for the responsibilities you have the next day. Curfews let us all know the boundaries, which will expand with the more responsibility you take. If there's a problem with a curfew on any night let us know.

In addition to setting curfew times, some parents have additional reasonable rules:

- We need to know where you are and who you're with.
- We need to know when you're leaving for home, especially if you're delayed. And if there is any problem with the car, we need to know who you're with, what happened and so on.
- You can call us at any time of the night, and we'll come to get you.

• It is true that some of your friends may not have a curfew or these guidelines to follow. It's all right, though. We do, and we care.[8]

Tattoos and Body Piercing

When the word "tattoo" is mentioned, what comes to your mind? What feelings does this word evoke? When the phrase "body piercing" is mentioned, what comes to your mind? What feelings do these words evoke?

Do you realize you have the right to say no? You as a parent are legally responsible for your child until he or she is 18. Even if your teen doesn't bring this issue up now, what will your teen do when he or she is of age? Do you ever want your child to get tattoos or pierce his or her nose, lip or tongue? It could happen. This is a time to educate your teen so that he or she knows not only your beliefs but also the social and health implications. There are consequences involved with tattoos and body piercing. Tattoos and body piercing are a reflection of a teen's search for identity and desire for acceptance. This is why it's important for children and teens to discover their identity and security in Christ.

Be open to discuss some of the short-term and long-term side effects of tattoos and body piercing with your teen. Short-term side effects include sleep, eating and speaking disruption due to healing; no swimming; no direct exposure to the sun for two to four weeks during the healing process; infection; pain; and risk of HIV and hepatitis.[9]

Long-term side effects include disliking tattoo or body piercing due to changing fashions, tastes and life circumstances; social rejection; difficulties finding a job; scarring; fading and stretching of tattoo; painful, expensive removal procedures; and wrong name in your tattoo for your current relationship.[10]

Some parents suggest temporary, removable tattoos, as well

as clip-on or magnetic rings. If your teen is pushing for a tattoo or body piercing, realize that your teen most likely has not thought through the risks, consequences and procedures.

Use these questions and comments to engage your teen in discussing the topic of tattoos and body piercing:

- Tell me what you like about tattoos and body piercing.
- I'm sure you've talked to those who like their tattoos and body piercings. What is the purpose of either? I'd like to know.
- Who have you talked with who doesn't like it or who wished they hadn't done it? It's important to talk to those on both sides of the fence.
- Personally, I don't find either attractive, and I'm concerned about using one's body in that way.
- How much do you know about the pain involved in getting tattooed or having them removed? What about the pain of piercing body parts?
- Tell me how you think this will affect your life.
- If we as your parents came home tattooed and with our lips and nose pierced, how would you respond? Remember, you will be our age one day with children of your own.
- How will your life be better if you have tattoos or body piercings?
- I can understand you want to do this. But we are against you doing any tattooing or piercing that will change your body permanently. When you're 18, you can decide. We believe the Scripture teaches that our bodies are temples of the Holy Spirit, and we need to honor what we do to our bodies, as well as what we put into our bodies (see 1 Cor. 6:19-20).[11]

DISCUSSION STARTERS

You can use the following questions with your child or teen to develop a conversation. Be sure to listen carefully. If you don't agree with what your teen says or believes, don't react or correct, or your teen may not respond at all the next time.

Sometimes we think we know what our children or teens are thinking; instead, ask them and let them speak for themselves. You may be surprised.

If your teen asks you what you believe about the same question, try to match the length of your answer with your teen's answer. This is not the time for lecturing or giving an earful.

Use the questions sparingly and try to weave them into everyday conversation. Some questions are more appropriate for teens. Sometimes we think we know what our children or teens are thinking; instead, ask them and let them speak for themselves. You may be surprised.

1. What are three things you like about your best friend?
2. If you could live anywhere else, where would it be?
3. What's the best time of the day for you? What's the worst time?
4. What do you wish your teacher would do differently?
5. If you could change one thing about this house, what would it be?

6. If you could ask God three questions, what would they be?
7. When you read something do you see pictures of it in your head or do you hear the words?
8. What do you remember most from five years ago?
9. What do you want to do five years from now?
10. What makes it easy to talk to others?
11. What were two of the questions on your test today?
12. What angers or upsets you the most at school?
13. What angers or upsets you the most at home?
14. What do you like and dislike the most at church?
15. What do you like most about the way you look?
16. What do you dislike most about the way you look?
17. Most of us have things we worry about. What do you worry about?
18. How often does bullying happen in your school?
19. What kind of clothes do you wish you could wear?
20. I need your advice on something. What do you think about . . . ?
21. What do you think I could do so that we could talk better together (or get along better)?
22. What do you think about the time of your bedtime (or curfew)?
23. Did I ever tell you about my first date?
24. Did I ever tell you about my first kiss?
25. Did I ever tell you about the time I was sent to the principal's office?
26. When you hear that someone died, what do you think?
27. When you see pictures of the planes flying into the World Trade Center what goes through your mind?
28. When you hear that a friend's parents are divorcing, what do you think?

29. What do you wish Jesus would do today?
30. What do you think about drinking alcohol?
31. What's the main reason your friends drink?
32. Do you think there are many kids in your school who use drugs?
33. What's it like for you when you succeed?
34. What's it like for you when you fail?
35. What do you wish we would do when you fail?
36. What's the hardest feeling for you to put into words?
37. How do you see others treating those who are gay?
38. What's the best thing you like about the Internet?
39. What's the worst thing you've seen on the Internet?
40. If you could play a musical instrument (or if you could play an additional instrument), what would it be?
41. In what way do you feel pressure from your friends?
42. There's a lot of sex on TV, movies and the Internet. What do you think about sex in the media?
43. What do you appreciate most about your pastor (or youth leader)?
44. What don't you appreciate about your pastor (or youth leader)?
45. Who would you say is a hero in your life?
46. When you drive, what will be your biggest concern?
47. What do you think about smoking?
48. What are the reasons to smoke and not to smoke?
49. Do you know what stresses you the most?
50. What's the best thing that's happened to you this year?
51. What do you think when you see someone who has a lot of body piercings?
52. Have you ever thought of getting a tattoo?
53. Have you ever asked your tattooed or pierced friends

to tell you about their experiences before and after the procedure?

54. If you could ask either of us any question you ever wanted to ask, what would it be?

Here are five scenarios. Read each one and describe what you would say. After you respond, read the worst and best responses for the same questions in table 7.1. Compare your responses to the worst and best responses.

1. Your teen's library book is a week overdue. Your response:

2. Your son's Sunday School teacher will be here in 10 minutes to pick him up for an outing, and your son is running late. Your response:

3. Your child's bike was left on the front doorstep again. Your response:

4. Your child's dog is out of food and water. Your response:

5. Your daughter has been playing with the little girl next door, but now it's time to come in and she does not want to. Your response:

Table 7.1

Responses

The Worst	The Best
1. "John, I can't believe you let that book go for a week. Take it back today. That is so irresponsible."	1. "John, the library book is a week overdue. What's your plan?"
2. "Hurry up. You should have planned more time. You're going to delay everyone. Get your coat, and if you're late tell them it's your fault."	2. "Your teacher will be here in 10 minutes."
3. "Get that bike off the front doorstep. How many times do I have to remind you? What's it going to take for your mind to remember?"	3. "The bike belongs in the garage now."
4. "You never remember your dog. How would you like it if we didn't give you food and water? If you forget it again, we may have to find a new home for her."	4. "Your dog needs water and food. I'd like you to come up with a way to remind yourself to do this."
5. "You had a good time. Don't spoil it by making a fuss. If you do, next time you won't get to play. Now, do you hear what I'm saying? Come in now."	5. "You had a good time playing, and now it's time to come in."

CURRENT LEVEL OF COMMUNICATION

It is important to gauge your current level of communication with your child or teen. Use an X to indicate your level of communication, with 1 meaning almost never, 2 meaning rarely, 3 meaning sometimes, 4 meaning often and 5 meaning almost always. Then use a circle to indicate what you think your child's or teen's level of communication is at the present time.

1. Listens when child (or parent) is talking

    1   2   3   4   5

2. Appears to understand child (or parent) when he or she talks

    1   2   3   4   5

3. Tends to amplify and say too much

    1   2   3   4   5

4. Tends to condense and say too little

    1   2   3   4   5

5. Tends to keep feelings to him- or herself

    1   2   3   4   5

6. Tends to be nag or critical

    1   2   3   4   5

7. Encourages child (or parent)

    1   2   3   4   5

8. Tends to withdraw when confronted

   1   2   3   4   5

9. Holds in hurts and becomes resentful

   1   2   3   4   5

10. Lets child (or parent) have say without interrupting

   1   2   3   4   5

11. Remains silent for long periods of time when child (or parent) is angry

   1   2   3   4   5

12. Fears expressing disagreement if child (or parent) becomes angry

   1   2   3   4   5

13. Expresses appreciation for what is done most of the time

   1   2   3   4   5

14. Complains that child (or parent) doesn't understand him or her

   1   2   3   4   5

15. Can disagree without losing his or her temper

   1   2   3   4   5

16. Tends to monopolize the conversation

   1   2   3   4   5

17. Feels free to discuss any subject openly with child (or parent)

   1   2   3   4   5

18. Gives compliments and says nice comments to child (or parent)

    1   2   3   4   5

19. Feels misunderstood by child (or parent)

    1   2   3   4   5

20. Tends to avoid discussions of feelings

    1   2   3   4   5

21. Avoids discussing problem topics or issues with child (or parent)

    1   2   3   4   5

SCORING KEY FOR YOUR CURRENT LEVEL OF COMMUNICATION

Statements 1,2,7,10,13,15,17 and 18

To determine your score, add the numbers you made an X through for each of these eight statements. The sum reflects your score. To determine your child's score, add the numbers you circled for each of these eight statements. The sum reflects your child's score.

Your score _____

Your child's score _____

      33-40   You're doing very well.

      25-32   You're doing well.

      17-24   Some areas need improvement.

      8-16   Definite improvement needed.

Any statements having a communication level of 3 or lower would benefit from some work. Any statements with a level of 1 may need outside assistance.

Statements 3,4,5,6,8,9,11,12,14,16,19,20 and 21
To determine your score, add the numbers you made an X through for each of these 13 statements. The sum reflects your score. To determine your child's score, add the numbers you circled for each of these 13 statements. The sum reflects your child's score.

Your score _____
Your child's score _____

      53-65   Definite improvement needed.

      40-52   Some areas need improvement.

      27-39   You're doing well.

      13-26   You're doing very well.

Any statements having a communication level of 3 or higher would benefit from some work. Any statements with a level of 5 may need outside assistance.

A Message from a Parent to a Child Embarking on Adolescence

Dear In-betweener,

Well, guess what? You've got one foot on the launching pad and one hovering over the launching pad. You're an in-betweener. Part of you has some roots remaining in childhood and part is flailing around for a place to settle in adolescence. It's an exciting time. It can also be a frightening time as well.

You're going to struggle at this crossroads in your life. You're faced with two roads to choose from. And you will have to decide which one to travel. One road will be very enticing—it offers you happiness and satisfaction based on circumstances. The other road offers you joy regardless of what happens.

One road will be very attractive with relationships that are not friendships. They carry hidden agendas and a price tag you won't know about in advance. The other road offers a simple uncomplicated love and acceptance.

One road will entice you with immediate thrills and pleasure, but the price tag may be addictions. The other road offers you peace and self-respect. You'll be able to hold your head up high.

One road is going to look attractive to you with its promises and vows, but they can be broken. Most likely, they will be. The other road offers you something that will never change and can always be trusted. The promises are true.

Finally, to help you in your choice, memorize these words. Feed upon them. They're your road map. Your direction finder. Let them speak to you:

Do not love the world or anything in the world. If anyone loves the world, the love of the Father is not in him. For everything in the world—the cravings of sinful man, the lust of his eyes and the boasting of what he has and does—comes

not from the Father but from the world. The
world and its desires pass away, but the man who
does the will of God lives forever (1 John 2:15-17,
NIV).

Your Loving Parents[12]

Chapter 1

1. Otto Kroeger and Janet Thuesen, *Type Talk* (New York: Delacorte Press, 1988), pp. 10-11.
2. John Gray, Ph.D., *Children Are from Heaven* (New York: HarperCollins Publishers, 1999), pp. 206-215.
3. Kroeger and Thuesen, *Type Talk*, pp. 33, 83, 93, 145.
4. Ibid.
5. Ibid., p. 33.
6. Marti Olsen Laney, Psy.D., *The Introvert Advantage* (New York: Workman Publishers), p. 152.
7. Ibid., pp. 69-70.

Chapter 2

1. Ray Guarendi, *Back to the Family* (New York: Villard Books, 1990), pp. 142-143.
2. Leonard Zunin and Natalie Zunin, *Contact: The First Four Minutes* (New York: Ballantine Books, 1972), pp. 150-152.
3. Ibid., pp. 154-155.
4. Guarendi, *Back to the Family*, pp. 145-147.
5. Denis Donovan, M.D., M.Ed., and Deborah McIntyre, M.A., R.N., *What Did I Just Say!?!* (New York: Henry Holt and Co., 1999), pp. 147-154.

Chapter 3

1. Matthew L. Linn and D. Linn, *Healing Memories* (Ramsey, NJ: Paulist Press, 1974), pp. 11-12.
2. Jean Illsley Clarke and Connie Dawson, *Growing Up Again* (New York: Harper and Row, 1989), pp. 53-61.
3. Robert Sherman, Paul Oresky, and Yvonne Roundtree, *Solving Problems in Couples and Family Therapy* (New York: Brunner Mazel, 1991), pp. 233-234.
4. Ibid.

5. For more information, read Tim Kremmel, *Grace-Based Parenting* (Nashville, TN: W Publishing Group, 2004).

Chapter 4

1. Naomi Drew, *Peaceful Parents, Peaceful Kids* (New York: Kensington Books, 2000), p. 30.
2. Nancy Samalin with Martha Moraghan Jablow, *Loving Your Child Is Not Enough* (New York: Penguin Books, 1998), pp. 122-123.
3. Ibid.
4. John Gray, Ph.D., *Children Are from Heaven* (New York: HarperCollins Publishers, 1999), pp. 38-40.

Chapter 5

1. Ron Taffel with Melinda Blau, *Parenting by Heart* (New York: Addison Wesley Publishing Co., 1991), pp. 166-168.
2. Paul M. Rosen, Ph.D., *TLC: Talking Listening Connecting* (Upper Saddle River, New Jersey: Alpha Books, 2002).
3. Ibid., pp. 57-58.
4. Ibid., pp. 44-54.
5. Ibid., p. 76.
6. Ibid., p. 115.
7. Denis Donovan, M.D., M.Ed., and Deborah McIntyre, M.A., R.N., *What Did I Just Say!?!* (New York: Henry Holt and Co., 1999), pp. 56-57.
8. Charles R. Swindoll, *Strike the Original Match* (Portland, OR: Multnomah Press, 1980), p. 92.

Chapter 6

1. For more information, read David Stoop, *Understanding Your Child's Personality* (Carol Stream, IL: Tyndale House Publishers, 1998).
2. Foster Cline, M.D., and Jim Fay, *Parenting with Love and Logic* (Colorado Springs, CO: NavPress, 1990), p. 83.
3. Nancy Samalin with Martha Moraghan Jablow, *Loving Your Child Is Not Enough* (New York: Penguin Books, 1998), p. 14.
4. Ray Guarendi, *Back to the Family* (New York: Villard Books, 1990), pp. 135-136.
5. Denis Donovan, M.D., M.Ed., and Deborah McIntyre, M.A., R.N., *What Did I Just Say!?!* (New York: Henry Holt and Co., 1999), pp. 7-8.
6. Robert Dilts, *Applications of Neuro-Linguistic Programming* (Cupertino, CA: Meta Publishers, 1983), pp. 3-15.

7. H. Norman Wright, *Pre-Hysteric Parenting* (Colorado Springs, CO: Cook Communications, 2001), n.p.

Chapter 7

1. Barbara C. Unell and Jerry L. Wyckoff, Ph.D., *Eight Seasons of Parenthood* (New York: Times Books, 2000), pp. 155-156.
2. Don H. Fontenelle, Ph.D., *Keys to Parenting Your Teenager* (Hauppauge, NY: Barron's Educational Series, 2000), p. 8.
3. Ibid., pp. 8-11.
4. Ibid., pp. 105-106.
5. Ibid., pp. 46-48.
6. Foster Cline, M.D., and Jim Fay, *Parenting Teens with Love and Logic* (Colorado Springs, CO: Pinon Press, 1992), pp. 239-240.
7. Richard Heyman, *How to Say It to Teens* (Paramus, NJ: Prentice Hall Press, 2001), pp. 3-4.
8. Ibid., p. 95.
9. Ibid., p. 417.
10. Ibid.
11. Ibid., pp. 417-419.
12. Archibald Hart, *Stress and Your Child* (Dallas, TX: Word Publishing, 1992), p. 142.

Relevant Reading
from H. Norman Wright

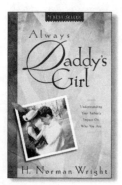
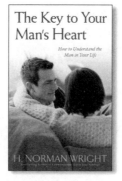